The 50s & 60s

THE BEST OF TIMES

Growing up and being young in Britain

ALISON PRESSLEY

This title was published previously in two volumes,
The Best of Times and *Changing Times*
and as a single volume in hardback.

Compilation copyright © 1999, 2000, 2002, 2003 by Michael O'Mara Books Limited
Text copyright © 1999, 2000, 2002, 2003 Alison Pressley

A CIP catalogue record for this book is available from the British Library

ISBN 978-1-84317-065-5

20 19 18 17 16 15

Edited by Yvonne Deutch and Gabrielle Mander
Designed by Design 23

Printed and bound in Italy by L.E.G.O., Vicenza

Alison Pressley is a book editor, writer and publisher. She was born in 1947 in South Shields, County Durham and was educated at South Shields Grammar Technical School for Girls, Kingsbury County Grammar School and Manchester University, where she gained a BA in American Studies in 1969. She left England in 1973 to travel the world via the hippie trail, and has lived in Sydney, Australia since 1974.

Picture Acknowledgements:

Front cover
Seaside image: National Railway Museum/Science and Society Picture Library
Sweetshop image: Lilian Ream Exhibition Gallery

Lilian Ream Exhibition Gallery:
p.23: top right; p.31: top right; p. 33; p. 56; p. 58; p. 79

Advertising Archives : 180 top, 216 top, 224
Corbis Bettman: 118, 123, 126, 131, 140 right, 142, 143, 150, 175, 188, 189, 190, 191, 196, 211, 213
Hulton Getty: 153, 154, 155, 179, 194
PA News Agency: 133, 143 right, 146 top, 158, 159 below, 222, 223
Popperfoto: 170-171, background, 172 top
Syndication International: 209 *Daily Express*
Courtesy of Richard Adams Associates: *Oz* cover, 164

Special thanks to Audrey Slaughter for the loan of her personal archive copies of *Honey* and *Petticoat* magazines.

The publisher would like to thank Ron Callow, Nigel Fountain, Richard Margrave and Judith Palmer as well as the author and the author's friends for the loan of personal photographs and memorabilia, and apologizes if the name of any individual contributor has been inadvertently omitted.

Acknowledgements

It will be fairly obvious to even the most casual reader of this book that it is based purely on personal recollections of the fifties and sixties. I have left historical research into statistics and hard facts to more formal and better qualified chroniclers. The idea of *The Best of Times* is to use people's memories – incomplete and flawed though they sometimes are – to build a picture of the decades through the eyes of their children and teenagers. I hope that the experiences described in these pages strike many chords with readers. My main debt is to author Helen Townsend, whose book *Baby Boomers: Growing Up in Australia in the 1940s, 50s and 60s* (Simon & Schuster Australia, 1988) provided the idea, the inspiration and the role model. I would also like to thank all the friends and relatives whose reminiscences make up the bulk of the text: Derek Barton, Wendy Canning, Jenny Cattell, Mavis Cheek, Tom Dack, Carol Dix, Joyce Foley, Peter Garland, Neal Gordon, Trevor Grove, Valerie Grove, Cliff Hall, Lisa Highton, Simon Hopkinson, Roy Jackson, Pat Kirby, Ray Kirby, Elaine Lister, Caroline Lurie, Heather McCauley, Frances McKenna, Janet Prescott, Jennifer Roberts, Tony Roberts, Rosalind Snaith and Judy Spittlehouse. They all submitted to my video camera with great good humour and made compiling this book enormous fun.

Thanks are due to my sister Valerie Grove for leaning on her famous friends to provide reminiscences which appear throughout the book as '*My Fifties*' and '*Days I'll Remember*'. Thank you also to those famous friends!

Finally, a huge thank you to Lesley O'Mara, Gabrielle Mander and Yvonne Deutch of Michael O'Mara Books for bringing the whole project to life

ALISON PRESSLEY

We'll talk of sunshine and of song,
And summer days, when we were young;
Sweet childish days, that were as long
As twenty days are now.

WILLIAM WORDSWORTH, *To a Butterfly*, April 1802

Foreword

You are amazed that the newsagent, who is aged about 27, cannot tot up the cost of three items, totalling one pound twenty, without a calculator. You remember having to calculate in your head how much a dozen eggs at twopence-three-farthings would cost. You remember farthings. You remember Liberty bodices, suspender belts, nylons, roll-on girdles, paper-nylon petticoats, winkle-picker shoes, crisps packets with little blue waxed paper twists of salt inside, Duffel coats, black Bakelite telephones with exchange names and simple numbers, the single plug-in wireless set shared by the entire family, the black Ford Popular car, the first 14-inch television screen around which the entire neighbourhood gathered to watch the Coronation, the first portable transistor radios.

You read the *Beano*, the *Eagle* and *Girl*. You remember Suez. You benefited from the Butler Education Act. You sat in rows of desks with lift-up lids and ink-wells. Your history classes were about kings and queens, your geography about capitals and the jute trade. Nobody mentioned global warming or the threat to the ozone layer; the only anxiety was the bomb – which could be banned, if you marched and sang loudly at the end of the decade. You went to the pictures on Saturdays. You bought 78 rpm records of Elvis Presley and Buddy Holly.

You are a Baby Boomer, born after World War II ended, just in time to enjoy the innocent, secure, never-had-it-so-good fifties. You had a really fab time at your twenty-first birthday in the swinging promiscuous sixties . . . You hit your fiftieth birthday in the nineties . . . and the Millennium finds you still in your prime . . .

VALERIE GROVE

Introduction

We were born into an innocent, optimistic world. Our parents had survived the horrors of World War II; the returning heroes, our fathers, came home to a world full of promise of better times to come. They were reunited with welcoming, lonely wives, and in a spirit of celebration and thanksgiving they conceived us – in unprecedented millions. We were the Baby Boomers, the fruits of joy after long separation. It was an auspicious beginning.

We were born in the years after the war, as Britain picked herself up, shook herself down and started all over again. In this world there was hardship, of sorts – but nothing like the Depression our parents and grandparents had endured. Rationing and shortages, to be sure, but also relative luxury: peace, and growing prosperity. Our world was one of trust, and neighbourly concern. We played innocently in the streets and parks of our neighbourhood, unmindful of the dangers that lurk today. They didn't exist, then.

We benefited from the Butler Education Act of 1944 and the construction of a 'Welfare State' in the late 1940s, and grew into the healthiest and most widely educated generation ever. Our early childhood was by today's standards austere, but by history's standards it was full of largesse. We thrived and prospered under the post-war expansiveness, and when we reached our teens towards the end of the fifties and the beginning of the sixties, we exploded.

We became this – and perhaps, to date, any – century's most influential generation. The 'Swinging Sixties' still reverberate, still make waves. Its leaders still lead – although we are growing rather long in the tooth. The generations after us are beginning to resent us and our lingering influence: 'Move over', they say, 'let us have our day.'

So, before we are swamped forever by the tidal wave of generations now happening and to come, let's have one more celebration of us, the lucky generation who grew up in the best of times, in the best of places. Mindful of the second half of the quotation that serves as the title of this book (Dickens's 'It was the best of times, it was the worst of times' which opens *A Tale of Two Cities*), it is here acknowledged that our childhood wasn't perfect – but it was as close to perfect as it gets. Here's a toast to the fifties – the decade that made us – and everything it brought, from the Woodentops to Elvis, from Liberty bodices to blue suede shoes.

And what about the impact of the sixties on the lives of ordinary young people – kids from the provincial towns and suburbs like thee and me?

The sixties were the heyday of youth power. Those of us who were children in the fifties reached our teens and twenties in the sixties – and we found ourselves in the middle of a heady explosion of colour and sound and creativity the like of which our flabbergasted and frequently outraged parents had never seen.

Like most decades celebrated for their mood, their certain style, the sixties didn't really start until well into the decade, about 1963. Before then, the mood was very much that of the fifties. Rock music was still essentially pop; fashions were leftover Teddy boy and girl stuff; public morality was firmly entrenched in the traditional strict not-until-you're-married attitude. Then roughly when The Beatles first became popular, everything changed. The youthquake hit, and nothing was the same again, ever. In the sixties the times were, in all respects, a' changin'.

What was it like to be young in the sixties in Hull, Newcastle, Worcester, Farnham? Going to the first boutique to open in Birmingham… the frisson felt by London girls when the buzz about Biba got around… screaming at concerts in Wigan… doing the twist at dance-halls in Bolton… being persecuted by the headmaster because you dared to be the first boy at your school to get a Beatle haircut… taking that first puff of marijuana, or steadfastly refusing to do so… getting wheels, breaking loose, taking off…

The idea of the second part of this book – changing times - is to paint a portrait of a decade in a series of vignettes and anecdotes. Nothing heavy, nothing academic or anthropological. Just our stories. I hope you relive your own glory days as you read the funny, sad, touching and occasionally cringe-making reminiscences of twenty or so ordinary people who were young in Britain in the sixties. Our memories were shared by millions, and they accompany us as we gently f-f-f-fade away.

The Fifties Contents

'Are you sitting comfortably?

Then I'll begin...'

PART 1
Living with Mother

Daily life at home

In the fifties, just about every pre-school child in Britain stayed home with either their mother or an aunt or grandmother during the day. Hardly any mothers went out to work, so the daily minutiae of the household – cleaning, cooking, shopping, tradesmen, neighbours – was as much a part of our early lives as it was a part of our mothers' lives. By today's standards, houses were cold, uncomfortable and fairly spartan: at the beginning of the decade such things as refrigerators and television sets were unknown in the average house. Few households had cars, so the shopping was done locally, with rare trips into town or a nearby city, and tradesmen – including grocers and greengrocers – would come to your door. For us, as children, the life of the immediate neighbourhood loomed large.

Housework and household style

In retrospect the fifties heralded the new modernism in interior décor and household style – it was, after all, the decade that saw the unprecedented spread of washing machines, refrigerators and vacuum cleaners. But reality, for most of us, was a house that was a relic of the pre-war days: dark, unbelievably cold, and with primitive plumbing arrangements.

Housework in the fifties followed a rigid time-table, regardless of the weather or anything else. Mondays were washdays. Tuesdays, ironing. Dusting and polishing were always done on Thursdays, the big shop on Fridays. Nothing whatsoever was done on Sundays – except, of course, vast amounts of cooking and washing up.

The sound of the vacuum cleaner was so depressing. As was the sight of my mother in her turban and pinny. She spent all day cleaning on Thursdays. Our furniture was all 'utility' furniture, very plain: square tables and armchairs, of no distinction.

After the weekly wash was done on Monday morning it would as likely as not rain, so the dining room would be filled with clothes horses draped in wet washing, completely obscuring the gas fire. The clothes would steam gently and we would sit frozen behind them. I hated wet Mondays.

Everybody did everything in the room where the fire was, in the winter. That was the only room that was halfway warm, except for at Christmas maybe. Going to the toilet was agony, it meant going out into the rest of the house, where it was always freezing.

Every room in our house was so cold. The kitchen with the range was the only really warm room; everywhere else had lino-covered floors, with the occasional rug, and a runner in the hall. It was like living in the Arctic Circle.

Our front room was never used. It was kept pristine and only used on formal occasions, which was hardly ever. It seems crazy now, the house was so small. We all sat crammed into the kitchen. But that was the way, then.

I remember going to my grandmother's house and noticing how quiet everything was. You could hear the clocks ticking, and papers rustling. I seemed to spend a lot of my childhood waiting for things to happen, and hearing quiet things: clocks ticking, birds singing. You couldn't go down and watch television if you woke up before the grown-ups, like kids can now.

We used to love going to our grandmother's house. She had a washhouse in the garden with a huge tub and a poss stick or plodger and a dolly blue and a washboard. It also had a dartboard, so invariably one of us would end up with a dart in our leg.

You've finished your wash— but is it only half done?

However well you wash your clothes, the final results still depend on the wringing. And only Acme wringing makes it certain that washday after washday your clothes will be as clean, crisp and sparkling as ever you could desire. Five million women already know this. Whether they use a washing machine, sink or tub, they all say . . . .

However you wash— you should have

ACME wringing

ACME WRINGERS LIMITED DAVID STREET GLASGOW SE

Washing clothes was very labour intensive. Everything was washed in the one sink – kids, dishes, clothes. Mum did a clothes wash every day, without any mechanical assistance. The only piece of machinery was a mangle, a wringer. I tried very hard to put my fingers in it, and of course succeeded eventually.

Our weekly wash was done in the scullery, with a washboard and a mangle. The clothes were then hung outside on a clothes line, with a huge clothes prop to hold the line up. We didn't get a washing machine until the sixties.

Having a bath was such torture in winter, when anything out of the water froze, especially your back. And there wasn't that much water in the tank, either. Sunday night was bath night, so we'd have this terrible fire blazing all through the day on Sundays in summer, so that we could have a bath in the evening. It was hell.

Friday nights were bath night, and the tin bath would be brought in from the outside and filled with kettles of water. You had to get out of the tub on the coal fire side, because if you got out on the non-fire side you would simply die of cold.

My first baths were taken in the kitchen sink. It was a big, deep porcelain sink, as they all were then. Later on, when I was about four, we got a tin tub we used to keep out in the yard and pull in on bath nights.

Wash day is child's play!

It's goodbye to those wash day blues when you wash with one of Mr. Therm's NEW WASHING MACHINES! No hot water worries — Mr. Therm sees to that! The water is heated by Gas in the machine. You can have it boiling if you like! Then it's power agitated — and the washing's over in no time! Quiet, economical, efficient—thanks to Mr. Therm. See the latest Gas-heated washing machines at your Gas Showrooms—they're all on the easiest possible terms

Mr THERM burns to serve you

SIMON HOGGART
My Fifties
(B. 1946)

Scratchy grey flannel shorts and long socks with a ruler pushed down the right leg. Party telephone lines, so you could eavesdrop on neighbours' conversations. Never enough sweets because of rationing. Ford Consuls and Zephyrs – the first cars whose boots stuck out as far as their engines. AA patrolmen saluting. Cars whose suspension made you sick after twenty miles.

We had a dark, dank cellar where we kept our coal, and we used to keep our eggs in there too, in this great big china bowl, really huge – to me it looked like a small swimming pool – and the eggs were kept in this stuff called isinglass. I mean, now you just put them in the fridge, but we had to go down into this damp, dark cellar and put them in this liquid stuff. I used to think it was weird even then.

Part of the 'baby with the bath water' modernization of the fifties was people getting rid of their pianos. They would pay people to come and chop them up and take them away. I remember thinking at the time how awful this was. China went out, too – lots of really nice things. If you had a really nice old panelled door, you had to put hardboard over it, with beading all around. Same with fireplaces. Then you'd invite people in to come and look at the desecration. It was a real status symbol.

I remember those long, deep, cold stone sinks, scullery-type sinks with horrible bits of curtain under them, and cold stone floors. So some of the new fifties things were in fact improvements – warmer lino on the floor, nice new aluminium sinks and so on. But fifties kitchens were still really primitive. Hideous formica, and spiky-legged tables and things.

From the age of three until the age of nine – from 1950 to 1956 – I shared a room with my grandmother. I slept in a cot. My parents and my great-grandfather slept in two other rooms in the house, and we all lived in the only other room, the back kitchen. After that, we got a council house and I had a room to myself.

We used to keep our coal in the cupboard under the stairs. You'd take the coal-scuttle and use a big scoop to fill it with coal. One day when I went to fetch the coal there was an enormous toad sitting on top of the pile. I nearly screamed the house down.

I had to have a bath twice a week, which I thought was a bit of an imposition, with Lifebuoy soap which had a picture of a boy's face on it briefly before it turned into a hideous slimy sludge. Every other night had to be a DGW, which meant a Damned Good Wash. My mother would check me, and if I didn't pass inspection she would just dip the flannel – which was pretty rough – into the now-cold water and scrub vigorously behind my ears and neck and so on. I do it now to my own children, despite their cries of 'Mummy, don't!' Because you just see a child as some kind of wall with dirty marks on it.

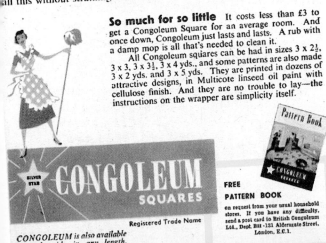

We had a stone shelf in the pantry, and a meat safe with wire mesh over the front. Things didn't keep very long in the summer, though, so my mother would shop just about every day for perishables.

We had a pantry with an opening to the outside, covered in a sort of grille. Everything was kept on the shelves in that. It kept food pretty well, really. But Mummy still went shopping every day — twice a day, sometimes. And my sister and I would have to run errands all the time, when we were old enough. Most perishable food was bought on a daily basis. Tiny amounts. My uncle had a greengrocer's shop and he used to sell half an onion, or one apple, quite regularly.

As a very young child I was terrified of the woollen army blanket that covered my bed. They were the only bedclothes available after the war, but they were scratchy and grey — totally alien and threatening.

Progress in the Home

Hoover Limited take pride in the fact that their products are saving millions of housewives from hard, wearisome drudgery — not only in Britain but throughout the world. Wherever the name Hoover appears it is a guarantee of excellence.

THE WORLD-FAMOUS HOOVER CLEANER

The Hoover Cleaner, with its famous triple-action principle — " It beats . . . as it sweeps . . . as it cleans " — is undeniably the world's best cleaner — best in design, best in materials, best in quality of workmanship. T is a model suitable for every size and type of home.

THE MARVELLOUS HOOVER ELECTRIC WASHING MACHIN

The Hoover Electric Washing Machine has completely revolutionised the whole conception of washing-day in the home. It does the full weekly wash for a large family and yet is such a handy size—suitable for even the smallest kitchen.

VISIT THE HOOVER FACTORY

Visitors to the Festival of Britain are cordially invited to make a tour of the Hoover Factories at Perivale, Middlesex, or Merthyr Tydfil, South Wales, or Cambuslang, Scotland. Please write to, Hoover Limited, Perivale, or 'phone Perivale 3311 for more information.

HOOVER LIMITED

Factories at :

ERIVALE, MIDDLESEX · MERTHYR TYDFIL · HIGH WYCOMBE · CAMBUSLANG, SCOTLAND

We had featherdown mattresses and quilts, and featherdown pillows; god knows what they did to your back, but they were immensely cosy to snuggle into.

I remember when a fitted carpet was installed, it seemed so modern. And when our first fridge arrived, and when we stopped having a plug-in radio. When our Electrolux vacuum cleaner arrived, long snaky thing, it was the last word in contemporary style.

Toilet paper in the fifties was revolting. We used stuff called Izal Germicide, which had the consistency – and the absorbency – of tracing paper, and smelt disgusting even before you'd used it. It came it nasty little cardboard boxes which took ages to fit into the metal holder, and each leaf was separate. You had to use at least half a dozen leaves to approximate a mass that would absorb any moisture at all – never mind anything else.

Mealtimes

**Parents just after the war made sure that their
children were well-nourished – almost too well-
nourished – so they'd weigh up well at their next
visit to the clinic. So families ate four meals a day,
consisting of a cooked breakfast and a cooked
meal at lunchtime, for many the main meal of the
day and often called 'dinner'; then there'd be
afternoon or 'high' tea, then supper.**

We had bread fried in lard or dripping, which we
called 'dip bread', for breakfast. It had to be really
greasy before we were satisfied. I remember my
sister saying scathingly 'Some people call this dip
bread!' at a particularly dry piece she was given.
It's a wonder we didn't die of heart failure at the
age of eight.

It was terribly important to my mother that
we always had a cooked, three-course
breakfast: cereal, then bacon and eggs, then
toast. Today it would be a killer, but at the
time it seemed desperately important.

I was constantly made to drink an egg-in-milk – a cup of milk with an egg broken into it, whisked up – because it was supposed to be good for me. I thought, 'I hate this, I can't drink it', but I had to.

The packets of cornflakes we had for breakfast sometimes had little plastic gizmos in the bottom. I remember one was a little submarine you put baking powder in, and it went down and came up again. It really worked.

'Snap, crackle, pop' was a harbinger of the new order of things. New cereals, new advertising. Ready Brek was another.

We used to walk home from school every lunchtime to have a meal, which we called 'dinner'. I remember standing at the back door and sniffing hard. If I could smell mince and potato – which I often could – I would refuse to enter the house.

The highlight of coming home from the swimming baths after the Splash Club on (usually freezing) Thursday nights was stopping off at the fish and chip shop for four penn'orth of fish and chips – with the *piece de resistance*, extra batter bits from the fish pan.

Make sure of a good meal

with a traditional plate of

Fish & Chips

Henry Morgan—President of the National Federation of Fishfriers — has championed the cause of higher standards in fishfrying for many years.

READ ABOUT FISH & CHIPS
on page 195

So Economical!

Buy Fish Tomorrow!

THE CHEAPEST FIRST-CLASS FOOD MONEY CAN BUY!

I had school dinners from day one because they were very cheap, but the food wasn't up to much. It was brought to the school in huge steel containers, so it was already congealed. The supervisor insisted that everyone clean their plates, and we had a dreadful piece of meat every day, full of fat and gristle, although I suppose that was all there was, after the war. She would look under the tables and everything, determined that every child should eat every morsel. So when I was about six I devised a clever system. I took two handkerchiefs to school each day. One was for blowing my nose, and the other was for taking the meat scraps home and dumping them in the bin.

School dinners were terrible. It took me years before I could eat cabbage after I left school, because when they took the lid off the stainless steel containers the smell of the cabbage was nauseating.

I was always envious of my friend up the road because she had supper, which consisted of a packet of crisps and a mug of Ovaltine. We had a cup of hot milk which I hated, not because of the taste but because of the vile skin that would always form on the top. You could blow it away to the other side of the cup but you always ended up getting some in your mouth. Ugh!

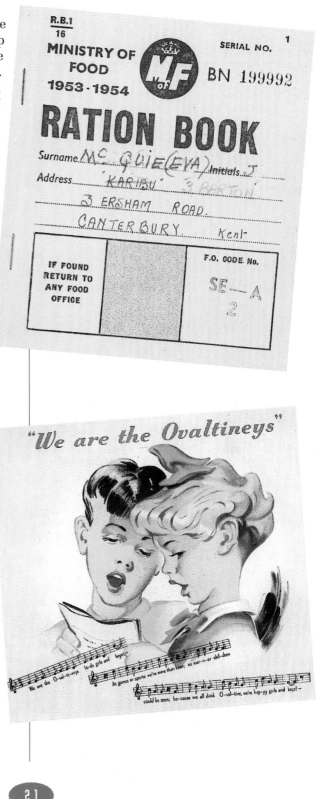

My Fifties

MAUREEN LIPMAN
(B.1946)

My crayons were kept in a mauve tin of Ostermilk. My hair was permed with Twink. My brother had an elasticated belt of red and green stripes with a snake clip. I didn't. I had a checked dress with smocking and puffed sleeves. He had Meccano and knew how long a furlong was. I had cut-out dolls from the back of *Bunty* and boxes full of cut-out clothes. He could make a face like the Mekon in the *Eagle*, which terrified me. We played out in the 'Tenfoot' until teatime, which was Heinz spaghetti on toast or an egg cooked in a saucer in the oven and called, imaginatively, 'saucer egg'. The TV, when it arrived, was a Bush 12-inch. Dad bought us a Dansette record player and three records: Edmundo Ros, David Whitfield and 'Itsy Bitsy Teeny Weeny Yellow Polka Dot Bikini'. Vimto was my tipple in the break at Muriel Riley's Ballroom Dancing Classes where I led Bernice Segal round the floor in a neat Valeta. Forty years later I still try to lead. In times of extreme stress I still resort to Heinz tomato soup and a slice of sliced white.

We seemed to eat an awful lot of jam. My father would make plum jam, blackcurrant jam. We had a big garden with lots of vegetables and fruit trees. He'd bottle a lot of fruit, too.

When I visited my childless aunt and uncle for afternoon tea we would have either fish paste sandwiches, cut into triangles, or salmon paste sandwiches, or pink salmon sandwiches, followed by Libby's fruit salad with Carnation milk. I still remember swishing the Carnation milk around the fruit salad, and getting that little grape – because we didn't have that much fruit then, other than apples. Even oranges and bananas weren't that prevalent. And of course it was all strictly seasonal.

We always walked home for lunch, nobody stayed at school for lunch unless there was something wrong with them, because why wasn't their mother at home looking after them?

Food in our house was an absolute ritual. If you asked me what I had for dinner on the first Monday in 1950 and the last Friday in 1959, I would be able to tell you. Because Sunday was a beef joint, with a monumental, plate-sized Yorkshire pudding filled to the brim with gravy; Monday was cold beef, and Tuesday was beef stew. Wednesday was sausages and mash; Thursday was rabbit pie; Friday was fish – and I can't face fish now because of all those Friday dinners – and Saturday was sandwiches, eaten on the run before the football match or the cricket.

Mackintosh's Rolo *Regd.* Rolo

CREAMY TOFFEE CENTRE

RICH MILK CHOCOLATE COVERING

in the Perfect Pocket Pack

"Shh! Stop Tommy! I think Mummy's coming up with our OXO."

OXO CUBE FOR A TASTY AND NOURISHING HOT DRINK

ENJOY THE STIMULATING PROPERTIES OF PRIME BEEF

Throughout the entire fifties we had only one meal: mince and mashed potatoes, with stewed apple and custard for pudding. We never went out to eat, and when we went on outings we took sandwiches made with bloater paste or Spam, and sometimes one of those fruit pies in cardboard boxes.

People used to mix butter and sugar together as a substitute for cream, which you just couldn't get unless you paid a fortune. It was called buttercream, I think. I never liked butter so I thought it tasted revolting.

Our grandmother used to churn her own butter. It was very scarce in those days, so she'd buy milk and churn it forever until she had butter. She was quite resourceful.

I remember lots of bulky foods. My favourite pudding was Spotted Dick, with lots of that revolting golden syrup, or treacle or custard. Of course it was just flour and water with a few raisins bunged in, boiled up in an old stocking or something. We always had plenty of rice puddings, because my Dad was the caretaker in a school and not all the kids drank their school milk, so we got all the leftover bottles.

We had terrible desserts, like rice pudding, tapioca, semolina. I hated all of them. Summer was all right, when we ate the fruit from our own trees, but winter was awful. Just like school dinners.

Our mother, like all mothers then, made a lot of cakes. We used to hang around the kitchen waiting until the mix was in the oven, then we could spoon and lick the mixing bowl clean. The taste of the mix was glorious, no matter what the type of cake, but neither my sister nor I cared for the cakes themselves. We always claimed they were 'just crumbs stuck together'.

I had a much older brother who was also of an age to be at the pub instead of home in time to eat the Sunday lunch. So there was always some recalcitrant male not doing his duty.

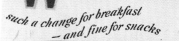

The drama would start early every Sunday morning. We'd get up and listen to Jean Metcalfe and Cliff Michelmore in 'Forces Favourites', which was as much a part of the Sunday ritual as having to peel potatoes and do sprouts and carrots.

We measured the Sunday cooking by what was on the radio. 'The Billy Cotton Band Show', 'The Navy Lark', 'Movie Go-Round'.

Vegetables seemed to go on for at least an hour. A lot of pea-shelling happened, then the peas were killed by overcooking like everything else.

Roast lamb had to be accompanied by mint sauce. I was in charge of collecting the mint from the garden and making the sauce, which consisted of equal parts of mint, sugar and brown vinegar, with a little bit of boiled water but not much. There was always a good slurpy bit down the bottom.

On Fridays we had real fish: kippers, and haddock poached in milk. To this day, I think things poached in milk look like someone's already eaten them.

Puddings involved cooking: Queen's pudding, angel cakes, rice pudding, caramel pudding, semolina. I could throw up at the thought of them.

When we were bought a packet of crisps – a rare treat – the real excitement was finding how many salts you had. Salt came in a twist of blue waxed paper, supposedly one per packet of crisps, but occasionally you'd get a windfall of three or even more twists of salt. And of course you had to use the lot, so if you did get the jackpot you'd end up with almost inedible crisps, slathered in salt.

Rationing was a great excuse for mothers. Whenever you wanted sweeties – just about every shopping trip – back would come the dreaded words, 'We haven't enough coupons left.' Nothing you could do about that, no matter what sneaking suspicions of perfidy lurked in your mind.

I remember the sweetie ration book, which was very real, and the day rationing was removed and I was able to go and buy a Mars bar. I got tuppence a week to spend on sweeties. All the sweeties in the sweetie shops were in jars, and you could get an awful lot of combinations for your money. You could get four blackjacks or four fruit salads or a Barratt's sherbet fountain with a stick of liquorice in it, or Pontefract cakes. Liquorice allsorts. Raspberry drops. Dolly mixture. Gobstoppers. Sherbet lemons. Toffee. All four for a penny – a farthing each.

I'd get sixpence a week pocket money, and I'd go up to the local shop on my trike and I'd get a penny sherbet, some fruit drops, then for

...such a DELICIOUS CHANGE!

CLARNICO *Regency Candi*

Masterpiece of flavour!

JOCKS LOVE SPANGLES...

("Awfu' guid sweets... and they last longer!")

DOC'S LOVE SPANGLES...

(Neatly wrapped, neatly packed ...and so refreshing)

STILL-LIFE ARTISTS IN SMOCKS LOVE SPANGLES...

("Oh, how those rich, fruity flavours inspire me!")

Assorted SPANGLES

ONLY 3d. A PACKET

AND YOU'LL LOVE SPANGLES

Wonderful new fruity sweets–made by MARS

ROWNTREE'S FRUIT GUMS

Taste the fruit!

When the advertisement for Rowntree's fruit gums came out, with the little boy shouting 'Don't forget the fruit gums, Mum!' after his departing mother, we were shocked and amazed that any child would be pushy enough to demand sweets every time his mother went shopping.

I had my own ration book, although I don't remember my things being rationed. Daddy's tobacco was, though. We used to go down to Mr Greenfield's and get a tobacco called 'No Name's' which came from under the counter.

tuppence I'd get Barratt's sweet cigarettes, so I could pretend to be smoking on my way home. They were made of sickly white stuff with red ends. Then I'd get a penny Spanish, or liquorice, or a penny pipe. The pipe was a bit of Spanish with a thick bowl on the end with red stuff in it, like those bobbly liquorice allsorts.

I remember how a Mars Bar, which cost fourpence, was a fantastic treat, and we had to share it between the four of us. The knife used to slice through the bar with such precision, in four equal parts. You got about an inch of Mars Bar each.

Parents

Parents in the fifties were regarded with a kind of awe by their children. We treated them with respect and we would hardly dare think of answering back. They told us what to do, and we did it. That was simply the way it was, then.

Mothers were godlike creatures in those early years. I don't remember seeing fathers much at all, but mothers were the Voice of Authority. You

didn't dare disobey their orders, or talk back to them, or cheek them in any way.

All mothers in those days carried handkerchiefs. And the minute you had the tiniest speck of dirt on your face, out would come your mother's hankie, on would go her spit, and your face would be rubbed vigorously with this horrible scentybreathy-smelling thing. It really was an objectionable habit. Thank God for tissues.

Just about everyone got smacked in the fifties. I can't remember hearing of any parent who was a conscientious objector in that field. A smart clip round the ear for boys and a smack on the bottom for girls was the norm, and no one seemed to think it cruel at all.

If we were doing something we shouldn't as children, my mother would say, 'If you don't stop doing that I'll run away with a black man.'

Adult men in the northeast all spat in those days, although 'Spitting prohibited' notices were beginning to appear in public places. My grandfather once famously spat into the ear of a passing girl, and had to give her half a crown. My father managed to spit into one of my school shoes, kept in the scullery, one day. I only found out, of course, when I put it on.

My father was a railway clerk, and he taught us not to believe in God, not to dance or read novels – 'a complete waste of time', according to him. I don't know what his motivation was, when I think about it now. Maths was okay, though. So I always got 'A's in maths.

My mother was always terribly conscious of, and proud of, the fact that my sisters and I had our own bedrooms. This was really important to her, because she'd had to share a bedroom with several siblings during her own childhood.

Daddy was omnipresent in our family. He used to cycle home for lunch every day from work. He was on a salary, not a wage, which was a very important distinction to our mother.

It was really important to my mother that she was the homemaker. The house we moved into in 1950 was a brand new house, built on a bombsite. It was the most wonderful house Mummy had ever lived in – everything was clean and new. She'd lived in dirty, miserable, horrible old houses all her life, and it was so exciting to her to move into this modern house, with a brand new bathroom. In 1958 we moved into a period house, and I know she was really sad even though it was a lovely old house.

It was terribly important to my parents that we were the archetypal happy family. They would get involved in our school, go to parent-teacher evenings, always come to everything we were in, do the school fete. They were scrupulous about it: you had to keep your children warm and safe and fed and clean and cherished. I think it was because so many families had been destroyed by the war.

My mother didn't go out to work, but every day she would shop, scrub clothes, dust, sweep the floors and cook. It was a full-time job then, keeping a house with children. She didn't sit around nattering to her friends or anything like that.

JON SNOW (B. 1947)

Blue screw-topped bottles of rationed orange juice.
Eggs in waterglass. Talk of war, and fear of it, contrasted with a life in the country of back-lit innocence. Long sunny afternoons, apples in the orchard and tree-houses with walls of hazelnut twigs and bulrushes whose cotton wool heads made us sneeze.

I don't remember Dad any more than most fifties children remember their dads, other than for what he failed to do. I remember him failing to take me places because we never got further than the pub – with me being plonked on the doorstep of the pub with a soft drink and a packet of Smith's crisps, promising not to tell Mummy. One time I wanted to go to the beach very badly, and I had my little ruched spotty bathing suit on under my clothes, which made you feel as though you were wrapped in a carpet roll, and sitting there the whole time and never getting to the beach at all because I couldn't pull him out of the pub. I was so cross with him, and I couldn't tell my mother, so I slammed upstairs which was all I could do.

My father used to stand in front of the range in the kitchen, where we more or less lived because the front room was for best, and say 'God, this is hot' while the rest of us froze because he was standing in front of the only source of heat, blocking it out, while we huddled on those brass fender seats.

My mother went out to work in a munitions factory, and I remember being truly mortified because she wasn't at home to look after me like other mothers. I'd sit in the bus stop, age five, waiting for her to come home every night.

Tradesmen

Home life in the fifties was punctuated by the arrival of endless home deliveries. This was quite normal, and was not reserved for the well-off.

When the milkman, or the rag and bone man, or any number of itinerant salesmen with horses and carts went by, all the women in our street would watch from behind their net curtains. If the horse crapped, they'd all rush out with their shovels and bags. Some almost came to blows, so prized was the fresh steaming stuff, especially for roses.

We'd have all our groceries and greengroceries delivered by Bill in his motorised van. We never bought anything from a supermarket — well, there weren't any, really.

You only ever see door-to-door brush salesmen depicted in cartoons these days, but they existed, and I felt sorry for them even as a child in the fifties. Such sad specimens, with their boring wares displayed on a tray in front of them, like the ice-cream ladies at the cinema but not nearly so enticing. The best they could hope for was to sell your mother a hairbrush or a toilet brush or a shoe-brush each visit. I wonder if they scraped a living out of it? I suppose they must have.

The rag and bone man came down our street pretty regularly. He was a bit of a con-man, as I recall, and for a big pile of really good used clothes or blankets or whatever, you'd have the choice of a goldfish or a sixpence, but it saved you the bother of trying to get rid of the unwanted goods any other way, and it was exciting, bartering just like in an exotic market or bazaar. He'd come down the middle of the street on his horse and cart, shouting 'Any old rags and bones?' in a singsong voice, the words barely decipherable. It sounded like ennyoleraanbo. It was a sign of the times that you could always hear him, because there just wasn't any traffic noise.

The Kleen-e-ze MAN stands for satisfaction. SEE HIM WHEN HE CALLS! Household & Personal BRUSHES. POLISHES. HAND CREAMS. KLEEN-E-ZE BRUSH CO. LTD. HANHAM BRISTOL.

Ginger the milkman delivered milk to our neighbourhood with his horse and cart until the end of the fifties. Sometimes he'd let us travel with him for a while, the cart swaying thrillingly. It was much more exciting than rides at the funfair.

The coalmen were terrifying creatures, bright eyes gleaming out of faces completely blackened by coal dust. They would shoulder hundredweight bags of coal and heave them up the drive and into the coal-shed, bent nearly double under the weight, black dust billowing everywhere. They used to deliver about twenty bags at a time because we lived in a school, and they were notorious for keeping a couple of bags behind. My Dad would watch them like a hawk, and a few times it came to fisticuffs. That was their beer money on the side. It was a tough job, and they probably weren't paid all that well.

The pop man would come every Thursday. He had bottles with those great big contraptions on the top that would take your eye out if you weren't careful. Our favourites were dandelion and burdock, and American cream soda.

A mobile shop would come around the village. And the milk came in a horse and cart, driven by the village idiot. He was harmless enough, and it was a good job for him because the horse knew what to do, which houses to stop at.

The world around us

Cities and towns in the fifties were quieter and more 'rural', and many suburbs looked, and felt, just like the countryside does today. We had a lot of freedom to wander and play. As for current affairs: without television, our worlds were smaller and more circumscribed than those of children today.

Before we had pesticides and main roads and pollution, I remember the amount of wildlife around. Whenever you went out, you'd see things like a shrew running across the path; every pond would have frogs and newts; there were water voles living in streams, insects on the surface. The noise of the birds – it was almost tropical. That gave me an affinity with, an understanding of, nature.

I used to go for a walk every day with my father, after he came home from work, and that's where I learnt about birds, and trees, and wild flowers. There were so many birds in those days. Cuckoos would sing all day. We had twelve species that nested in our garden, including house sparrow, hedge sparrow, starling, spotted flycatcher, greenfinch, chaffinch, blue tit, great tit, blackbird.

I remember the sight of fields of buttercups and daisies, and the smell of fresh-cut grass. Lying in the grass, holding buttercups under each other's chins to see if we liked butter or not. And making daisy chains to wear as necklaces. The ones with fat stems were best, as they were easiest to make a hole in with your fingernail.

Our town had been badly bombed in the war, and the town centre was riddled with vacant lots – bombsites. We just thought of them as our playgrounds. The clifftops had lots of

lookouts, too, dug into the ground and lined with sandbags. They were like cubby houses, but unfortunately most of them stank, as vagrants would use them as dosshouses and toilets.

We always used to go to the local farm at haymaking time. The tractors had little seats on the back, and I would sit on the back with this blade inches away. The farmer would pay us village children threepence a row – allegedly – to turn the hay. But nobody ever got paid. We always had cold tea. I suppose nobody had Thermoses then. Half the village would be there. It was terribly dangerous. Haystacks were very unstable, and very big. Once I fell off the top of one and knocked all my teeth out.

I remember the smell of fog, laced with coal dust, in autumn. Burning leaves. The pea soupers in London, which were yellow and phlegmy to look at. The absence of sound.

The first time I stayed in the country, I had no idea that most roads didn't have street lighting, and that it could get so incredibly dark at night. It was very frightening. To see my cousins shoot rabbits and then eat them. To go into the river, which had eels in it. To see foxes. It was so foreign to a city child.

We didn't live in central London, but even so the smog was really exciting when it came. We lived five doors from the corner of the street, and Mummy always used to stand at the front door and wave to us. But on the mornings of the smogs, we'd lose sight of each other way before we got to the corner. The smog was like phlegm in the air. It was yellow, and very bright, and moved, and it smelt very strongly. It also deadened the sound totally. The silence was phenomenal.

I really remember the class system. Our street was a row of workmen's cottages, but we were surrounded by enormous houses with huge grounds and gardeners, and staff and so on. And none of their children were allowed to play with us. They didn't speak to us. The golf club up the road had a class system too, with separate clubrooms for rich members and poor members.

In my first year of high school in 1958, our French teacher asked us what our fathers (not our mothers) did, so that he could tell us the word in French. So everyone said 'My father's a teacher', 'My father's a doctor' and so on. My father was a bricklayer, and – this is the most shameful thing I've ever done – I was too ashamed to admit it. I made something

up. And when I got home that night, I couldn't look him in the eye. It was my first real political lesson, because I remember thinking at the time, 'Hang on, there's something wrong here.' He was my hero, he was the fast bowler in the village cricket team, and yet I was ashamed of what he did for a living.

In those days, a single unarmed policeman could challenge a group of teenagers and they'd all disperse quietly. Now, he'd be taking his life in his hands. But if you saw a policeman then you'd run for your life, whatever you were doing!

My grandfather worked in the local quarry, more or less as they did in the 1800s: we used to go down and wave at him from the side of the quarry, and he'd be wearing trousers and nothing else, just carrying a pickaxe to break the stone. Our village constantly heard the boom of the explosions, and the whistle at one o'clock every day.

My Fifties

SUE TOWNSEND
(B. 1946)
Choking on a gobstopper whilst laughing at a William book. The 'chapped' legs caused by the wet rims of one's Wellingtons. Roaming the countryside, damming streams, lighting fires. Swapping 'jewels' which we kept on a bed of cotton wool in a tobacco tin. Snotty cotton handkerchiefs. Collecting the coal in a coach-built pram. Nightmares about the H-bomb. Newsreel of Belsen. Having nits and worms. Walking three miles to school and three back. Sitting in the yard of a pub with a Vimto and a bag of crisps. White dog shit. Spitting onto mascara. Radio Luxembourg, Sugar Ray Robinson. Deep snow.

What we wore

In the fifties, children's clothes were essentially no more than scaled-down versions of adult clothes. Even tiny babies were dressed in fairly elaborate costumes. There were no romper suits, practical corduroy overalls, cute socks with funny motifs or slippers in the shape of animals. Clothes were fairly sombre and utilitarian, with the exception of nauseatingly frilly, frothy stuff for girls' formal wear. Boys were stuck in short trousers until their voices broke, no matter how bitter the weather, and many had to wear miniature suits, complete with shirts and ties, on formal occasions.

5 MERITS IN THE 'Liberty' BODICE
REG TRADE MARK

For children of all ages

★ *healthful knitted material.*
★ *easy-slip-on style.*
★ *tailored tape reinforcements.*
★ *unbreakable suspender buttons.*
★ *backed by over 50 years' reputation.*

You can't buy better—'Liberty' bodices are worth looking for! Made only by R. & W. H. Symington & Co. Ltd., Market Harborough.

Liberty bodices were the bane of my childhood. The rubber buttons were so incredibly difficult for a child's hands to do and undo, especially on a winter's day when your fingers were frozen stiff. And if the day grew warm, you steamed gently inside them like a loaf in an oven.

Our mother took my sister and me to a children's fashion parade in a theatre. The posh compere described one dress and the child model lifted her skirt to show 'panties to match'. We thought this was a scream, and to our mother's horror we got up and mimicked the model in the aisle.

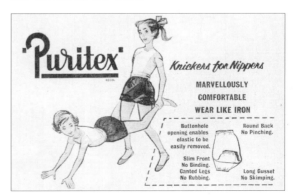

'Puritex' REG'D
Knickers for Nippers

MARVELLOUSLY COMFORTABLE WEAR LIKE IRON

Buttonhole opening enables elastic to be easily removed.

Round Back No Pinching.

Slim Front No Binding. Canted Legs No Rubbing.

Long Gusset No Skimping.

Smart dress was always a kilt, and a handknitted woolly. For parties, smocked dresses with cummerbunds. Being smartly turned out was hugely important to our mothers, and it was very pleasing for us too. I remember feeling terribly sorry for those children with runny noses and turned-down socks and scruffy shoes.

My sister and I were dressed in Little Red Riding Hood-type cloaks which we called 'doodie bonnets'. Anything, since, that has a hood or a peak is to me a 'doodie bonnet'.

I used to wear huge, bottle green bloomers with a pocket on the front right-hand side. I think it was meant for a purse or a hankie, but I never used it.

My mother was married in 1945 in a borrowed wedding dress, which always made her feel ashamed. But she went away on her honeymoon in a really nice jacket which was described in the local paper as a 'nigger jigger jacket'. I think it was astrakhan. She had it for years. Most people kept their clothes for years and years, then.

We always had to have a hankie with us, usually stuffed up a sleeve of our cardigan. They were always white, with embroidered flowers in one corner.

I liked to wear shorts – we wore Ladybird clothes, made out of Viyella. Little sweatshirts with V-shaped necklines, and little grey flannel shorts. I fell out of a tree once and tore them, so I was battling against the girl thing all the time. For occasions when we had to look smart, my mother made my sisters and me matching pleated skirts with little straps. I remember throwing an incredible tantrum because we were being taken to a cricket match and I wanted to wear my shorts, and I was forced to wear the pleated skirt like my sisters. I had to be manhandled into the car.

I remember wearing clothes for a long time, so that sometimes my skirts showed beneath my coat. There was a lot of letting hems down, and letting sleeves down – and you could never get rid of the crease.

"BUNNY and BALL" T-SHIRT
Cotton Interlock, in White, Biscuit and Turquoise. Sizes 2 and 4, price 4/11 approx.) Matching Briefs, 2/11 (approx.)

Ladybird

JEANS
Denim, sizes 2 to 14, prices 12/11 to 18/11 (approx.) With braces (sizes 2 and 4 only), in Navy, Red and Blue. Without braces: Boys' (zip fly), in Navy and Black; Girls' (side zip), in Navy, Black, Red and Blue.

LADYBIRD CHILDREN'S WEAR IS OBTAINABLE AT GOOD SHOPS EVERYWHERE

I got my first pair of jeans when I was about eight. Before that I'd had a pair of trousers for special, but apart from that I always wore short trousers. Every boy did. We didn't seem to feel the cold at all. We were always out running around.

I got a pair of jeans in 1956, when I was 10. They were very stiff, and not at all comfortable to wear, and they didn't look very nice. But I wanted a pair desperately, and had to bellyache for months until I got them. But for a long time afterwards, women and children didn't wear jeans – they didn't wear trousers.

In the mid-fifties the Brigitte Bardot look came in: tiny waists with wide white belts and huge frilly petticoats (we called it 'full-up net') under gingham skirts. The idea was to get the skirt as near to horizontal as possible. The petticoats always looked fabulous in the shops but once you put a skirt over them they lost all their oomph, and after they were washed they hung limply around your legs like a flag on a still day. I don't think my mother had ever heard of starch.

16

Blighty   April 27th, 1957

Blighty's Fashion Fanfare!

AS FRESH AS A DAISY
when you add a touch of white

This charming dress with its boat-shaped neckline, brief sleeves and full skirt becomes twice as attractive when you add crisply starched white pocket details and a curving band to the neckline. Make it up in a satinised cotton, pique, silky rayon or one of the new no-iron fabrics.
BLIGHTY-STYLE PATTERN No. 947 is cut in sizes 32, 34, 36, 38 and 40-inch bust. Size 36 requires 4½ yards of 36-inch material (skirt cut widthwise) plus ⅜ yard of 36-inch contrast.
To obtain this pattern, fill in the coupon on page 17 and send, with postal order for 2/6d., plus 3d. in stamps for postage and packing, to:—
BLIGHTY-STYLE PATTERNS, 64, FLEET STREET, LONDON, E.C.4.

BLIGHTY-STYLE PATTERN No. 947

I remember wearing a cap a lot. Not just at school, but at weekends as well. If a funeral went by you had to take your cap off.

My clothes were always too big for me, because they were hand-me-downs from my older brother. I've got short limbs, so I could never find my hands, and my 'short' trousers were down to my shins. I always looked grotesque, but I never minded because the thought of bothering about clothes or my appearance never entered my head. Getting dressed and undressed was just an interruption to having a good time.

I always wore Clark's sandals, in sensible brown, to school. I used to stare, fascinated, at the shape of the little flower pattern – and I liked to poke my fingers through the little holes and try and pull my socks through them. Apart from that we all just about lived in plimsolls (except we always called them 'daps').

We used to stick these steel things called Blakeys in the toe of our leather shoes. You'd hammer them in, they had cleats. They stopped you wearing out the toes of your shoes, but they made a terrible noise and they wrecked the floors of the school, so in the end they got banned.

I remember Tuf shoes were good when they first came out, they gave a six-month guarantee and had a vulcanised rubber sole.

When winklepickers came in in the late fifties my father wouldn't let me wear them, and I felt terribly isolated when I started secondary school. But I'm very glad now that I never wore them.

Church on Sunday meant wearing my best, and best was awful – it was clothes that just didn't fit me. I had to wear white gloves, with buttons at the wrist, and I hadn't to scuff my shoes, which had been whitened with some kind of stuff by me on Saturday night.

All women seemed to knit in those days, so we always had lots of jumpers. But my Mum wasn't the best knitter in the world, and I was sometimes embarrassed to wear the things she made. The boy down the road's mum was a brilliant knitter, and he had lots of Fair isle jerseys, things like that.

My much older cousin Kathleen wore little feathered half-hats and I thought them the last word in glamour. She and her friends wore dresses and suits with cinched-in waists and flared or tight skirts, hips swaying as they walked. As a beanpole eleven-year-old I longed to have broad hips I could swivel, and a big bum.

Nothing much changed from year to year. When you were ten, you assumed that the clothes you'd wear when you were fifteen would be the same as your fifteen-year-old cousins were wearing – but it fact it didn't work out like that, because just at the point where we turned teenage came the whole sixties explosion, and everything changed forever.

I hated all my clothes, because they were all hand-me-downs. Do you remember that ad, 'Gor-ray skirts, one better'? Well, forty years later I'm still tormented by that ad, because I wore a hand-me-down skirt to school one day and another girl sang this ad to me and I knew that she was really saying, 'That's a bloody awful skirt you're wearing'. So, yes, clothes were important in that they coloured a lot of things that happened to me.

Hair

Apart from the horrors of short back and sides, this section belongs to girls. We went through unimaginable torture to achieve the curls and ringlets favoured in the fifties, whether our hair was long or short.

Hair-washing nights were always a nightmare, because, the bathroom being so cold, you never wanted to expose flesh to it. I had really long hair, and there was no conditioner, so combing it out after washing was agony. I don't remember what type of shampoo we used, or even if we used any at all – was my hair washed in Lifebuoy soap, like the rest of me?

Our mother used to collect rainwater in the rainwater tank outside the scullery to wash our hair in, because it was softer than the lime-producing tap water where we lived. But it didn't help the horror of long hair being combed out afterwards.

You had to sit in front of the fire until your hair dried, which took forever, then you had to have it brushed out. That caused screams and anxiety enough. But then came the nightmare of getting it done up in rags – long strips of torn-up bedsheets – and I'd have to go to bed like some character in a novel, in my nightie, with these rags tied into my hair so tightly that it gave me a headache. I can still remember the pain. And my hair never retained the curl for long: it looked fabulous in the morning, then it would quickly fall out.

My mother wanted me to look my best for church on Sunday mornings, as most mothers did then, so she would get the curling tongs out and she would think it a good job done when I started yelling as the hot tongs were searing my scalp. The smell of burning hair lives with me to this day. They were very thin, mean-looking tongs and they had obviously done a lot of work as they were completely blackened from having been in the fire, or on top of the Aga where the kettle sat. My mother would wear protective gloves but my head, it seems, was an okay target.

I remember the real aching pain of having my hair scraped back into a bun or a pony tail, or even into plaits. It seemed that if a hairstyle didn't hurt, it wasn't worth doing.

You had to have your hair pulled, it was the norm. Your hair hadn't to have any tats in it. It was yanked every day. And your hair was only shampooed every fortnight, on a Friday. With Drene.

The smell of home perms stays with me from the fifties. My mother and her friends always seemed to be perming each other's hair in the kitchen, and the smell would strip paint. They used these little pink plastic rollers, like tiny bones, with paper wrapped round them. Sometimes our mother used 'setting lotion' on our hair, to force it into waves or curls.

There was such a thing as 'hair sore'. People would say, 'Oh, she's really hair sore.' And what it meant was that your hair was in such tatters that when you brushed it out it looked like rubbish.

Nits were a real problem because we all had such long hair. Suleo shampoo and Derbak combs were our best allies, although the latter crucified you.

You never made a special appointment at the local barber's, you always waited in a queue to have your short back and sides. Dad would always say, 'You're going for a Borstal slash.' So you'd come out with no hair, then a couple of months later you'd do it again. There was no concept of being able to organise your own life.

Pets

Pets were an important part of growing up after the war. With growing prosperity, some families could afford to take on extra mouths to feed in the shape of dogs and cats, but then, as now, budgies, goldfish, tadpoles and mice were also highly prized.

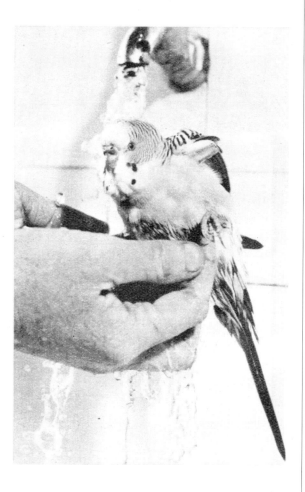

We had a budgie who had the curiosity of a cat. He was always nosing around everything, looking for food. One morning my dad came down into the kitchen and found Cheeky Boy in the frying pan, stuck fast. He must have been in the fat, eating the bits of leftover food, when it congealed overnight – which doesn't say a great deal for our cuisine in those days.

My mother used to tell us a silly story about a man with two goldfish called Ella and Emma. But I was terribly upset when my goldfish, Goldie – which I had received in exchange for some old clothes from the rag and bone man – died. My mother just threw the body on the fire before I got home from school. I had been deprived of digging yet another tiny grave in the back garden.

We used to put all the household food scraps into a container called a 'pig bin' in the back garden. The scraps were in fact intended for pigs, and the owner of the local farm would come and empty it once a week – if our dog hadn't beaten him to it.

Our next-door neighbour was a sea captain, and he came back from one trip with a monkey. Everything was all right until one day when it ran up the chimney – we all had coal fires – and of course then it was all over. It ran back down covered in soot and proceeded to scramble over everything. We didn't see it again after that.

I got my tortoise in 1953 and he cost me half a crown. I wanted to call him Jesus, but Mummy couldn't handle that so we called him Charles, after the Queen's son. I'm now on to Charles II.

We'd gather unfortunate creatures from the local pond and keep them in a murky jar for a few days, until they died or Mum told us to throw them away. Anything you could catch became a pet.

We kept tree frogs as pets and you had to feed them on bluebottle maggots. When we went away on holiday we left a load of maggots at the bottom of the cage. We came back after a fortnight, and as we neared our house Mummy cried, 'What's happened to the windows?' They were completely black – every single window in the house was black, covered in flies. All the bluebottles had pupated. For weeks and weeks, as you put clothes on, bluebottles would fall out.

Lots of people kept chickens. But we thought that people who had chickens in the garden were slightly common. Concrete was much classier.

WEEK ENDING OCTOBER 20 1951

EVERY WEDNESDAY

ILLUSTRATED

Juanita, The Gipsy Artist

4d. The Windsor Story—More Intimate Pictures From

THE DUKE'S ALBUM

Health care

The National Health initiative meant that post-war children grew up in a more healthy society than any previous generation. We had free school milk, subsidised orange juice, health and dental checks at school. But some childhood diseases were still killers. Poliomyelitis had one final devastating outbreak in 1955 and whooping cough, appendicitis and flu could – and often did – kill their victims.

Chicken pox and whooping cough and other childhood illnesses always had a quarantine period then, and you had to stay in bed for such a long time. You weren't even allowed to take your library books back during the quarantine period.

I had eczema as a child, which got infected and turned into impetigo, so I ended up with huge thick scabs all over my face. And I was terribly lucky, as it turned out, that this happened to me in the fifties and not in the sixties. Because by the time the sixties came along, the treatment consisted of dosing you with steroids. But I had to go to an isolation ward where they treated me by putting a thick mix of starch all over my face every night, covered with a tubular bandage with holes for my eyes. When I woke up in the morning the whole thing had set rigid. Then the nurses would come around with a trolley, with a huge bowl of calamine lotion. They would come into my room and grab hold of the bottom of this cast over my face and pull the whole thing off. With it would come all the scabs. Then they'd cover my face with the calamine lotion. My mother went bananas, convinced I'd be scarred for the rest of my life, but in fact it worked really well and fortunately I wasn't scarred at all.

We had all our injections, but I remember feeling unwell one year while we were on holiday. All sorts of doctors came to see me, but I was okay and went back to school when we got home. My mother told me years and years later that they'd been worried I might have polio. When I returned to school, the girl I'd sat next to the whole of the previous year had had polio over the summer. She was in irons as a consequence. Lots of children wore calipers then.

I used to get tonsillitis a lot as a child; it's amazing that they weren't taken out, but it was a stress-related thing and my doctor thought it was best to leave them in as a kind of built-in safety-valve, which was an incredibly enlightened view for the time. I would get very high fevers, 106^0 and such, and there was no penicillin at first; I was given this pale pink powdery liquid called Chorylmycetin. It obviously did the trick.

I remember people in our circle having polio in that 1955 polio outbreak. I heard of this thing called 'The Danger List' – I suppose you would call it intensive care now. The word 'polio' then was as frightening a word as 'cancer' is today.

Every time my sister and I became ill as children our family doctor would visit the house. There was no question about it: you were sick, you went to bed, and the doctor visited. Our family doctor was a hearty, jolly man who would invariably shout 'Plenty of jelly and blancmange!' as he left our house. We always groaned. We both hated blancmange, and didn't understand that this was meant to be a treat, not a treatment.

When I was eleven or so I heard a lovely rhyme from a boy in my class. It was a spoof of a then-popular ad for Andrews, the laxative. It went, "Do you wake up in the morning feeling as though the bottom's dropped out of your world? Take Andrews, and you'll feel as though the world's dropped out of your bottom!"

The universal cure for a sore throat or a cold in our house was butter, sugar and lemon. Our mother mixed these ingredients up on a plate or a saucer and spooned them into us whether we wanted them or not. The taste was not unpleasant but a bit sickly. It seemed to do the trick, though.

The school inspection was so dreaded. There'd be the nurse, who was always a battleaxe, and the doctor, who was always an old codger, and they'd say 'Drop your trousers and cough' and then they'd grab you. I dreaded it.

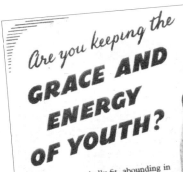

I hated the school inspections because you had to strip down to your vest and knickers and the doctor – who was always male – would pull the front of your knickers away from you and peer down them, presumably to see if you had pubes. Quite why they needed to know this escapes me.

Doctors in those days never told you anything. The trend over the years has been this change to open discussion, where they admit they don't know anything anyway. But I remember when you'd go in, and there'd be this chap who would always be in a suit and a waistcoat, heavy, authoritative, serious, and he'd never really look at you or smile or ask your name or anything. Your parents would say, 'Oh, he's got a pain in his stomach' or whatever, and they'd write a scrip with a squiggle, and that would be that.

It was really important then that you were fit and well. Mummy used to take us to the clinic, where there were posters about what time children should go to bed aged four, five, eight and so on, big posters on the walls showing smiling children.

We were given cod liver oil every day. Even now I gag at the memory. But the example of our dog, who would have killed for it, was held up in front of us. I recently bought some to convince myself that it wasn't so bad. It was even worse than I remembered – but my dogs loved it.

We had orange juice in glass bottles with blue tops. I remember taking the tops off and licking them.

There were red boiled sweetie medicine things, cherry flavoured, and they were disgusting. I still can't eat cherry-flavoured things. They were supposed to soothe sore throats.

I think cod liver oil was free. We'd get a bottle a fortnight. We'd also get orange juice concentrate. They said you needed malt extract

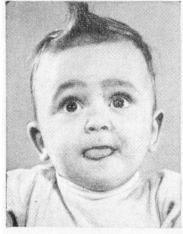
too, but they didn't supply that. Another 'cure-all' was rosehip syrup. And Scott's Emulsion, dreadful stuff that you took on a spoon. My grandmother swore by Lucozade, which she always brought round for us whenever we were ill. We didn't mind that at all.

It was terribly important to be clean, although we didn't change our clothes every day because there were so few washing machines, and no laundrettes.

Illness in the fifties always meant staying in bed and having the doctor visit you, and having a fire lit in the bedroom. A wonderful aura of calm and quietness, having all day to lie and read or listen to the wireless or colour things in.

Accidents

We had just as many accidents during childhood as previous generations. More, if anything, because we were freer to explore and therefore freer to come to grief.

I always had a bit of an aptitude for maths. I remember thinking hard about probability theory at the age of about seven. So I got this big half brick and threw it up in the air as far as I could, in the back garden, and I didn't look up on the basis that – by the laws of probability – it wouldn't land on me. Needless to say, about ten seconds later I was still standing there when there was this almighty wallop, right on top of my head. I spent three days in hospital. Hundreds of stitches. I've been bald ever since. I can't imagine children now being that naive.

I came off a pushbike and the side of my head was all smashed in. At the hospital they kept taking lots of X-rays, but they'd never do that now because of the danger of radiation. After our experiences in shoe shops, it's a miracle our feet haven't dropped off. Radiation was something that people just didn't understand then.

Children were forever getting their heads split open. I always thought this would be like an egg splitting open, and I was always surprised when I saw these children at school the next day with their heads still on their shoulders.

I have a scar over my left eye where a friend threw a cat at me. I asked him to do it; the cat was in a loft over his garage, and I said throw it down and I'll catch it. And of course it spread its claws out like that, and I did catch it.

Dental care

Dental care in the fifties was comparatively primitive, and fluoride was a distant dream. Most children in Britain had had several fillings by the time they reached double figures, and many had lost teeth. Anaesthesia was effected by administering gas through a face mask, and drills resembled road drills. As a consequence, dread of the dentist was almost universal.

We didn't get anaesthetic when we had fillings, that was only for extractions. And they had those awful low-speed drills. The sound alone was enough to send you into screaming fits in the waiting room.

Dentists in the fifties seemed to specialise in inhabiting dark, gloomy rooms full of clunky dark-brown furniture. They were like torture chambers, especially when suffused – as they usually were – with the smell of anaesthetic.

I remember a smell of rubber, which probably came from the mask they put over your face for the gas. And the horrible dreams you had after the gas. Torture chamber stuff. To this day, I can't bear anyone trying to put anything over my face.

The dentist was hell. 'I can see from my records, young lady, that you haven't been to see me for two years. It says here . . .' Everything was agony.

When I was 11 or so I had several teeth taken out because I had this terrific facial pain and it was just assumed that my teeth were the problem, that it was toothache. When the anaesthetic wore off, the pain was still there. It turned out to be my sinuses, but by the time they found this out it was too late, my teeth had gone.

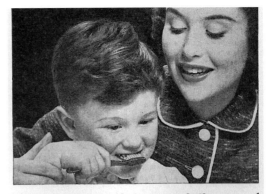

Every child of my age had their tonsils out, and their teeth out. Suddenly, when you were twelve or thirteen, someone – the dentist, I suppose – would say, 'They've all got to come out', and I remember it being a big macho thing: 'I've had ten out' or 'I've had thirteen out'; we'd boast about it.

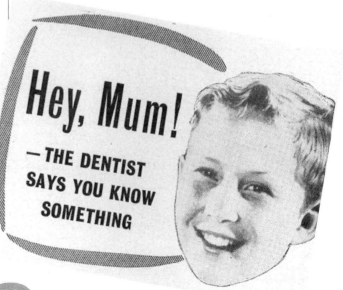

The happiest days ...schooldays

INFANT SCHOOL

Children in the 1950s started school at age five. Before then, we had lived at home so school came as rather a shock to the system – despite the fact that infant school was little more than a crèche for the first year or so.

I will always remember my first day at school. I was aged five years and three days, and I was tiny. Next door to me was a boy aged almost six, and he was huge. A monster. All I could think was that I was desperate to wee, and I didn't dare ask how or where to go. We were given a bottle of milk to drink through a straw, and I had to drink it, which made me even more desperate to wee. By the time I got home that lunchtime – I walked by myself – I was nearly dead. I've spent the rest of my life desperate to go to the toilet. But the really galling part of it was that I thought that once you'd done that stint at school, that was it. I was really shattered to discover that I had to go back that afternoon.

I remember my first day at school, sitting on the desk and crying and crying and crying. Crying all day. Leaving home was the worst hell I could possibly have imagined. Then suddenly, Miss Beverley called us all to sit around her and listen to a story, a Brer Rabbit story. This was a magical turning point in my life. She calmed me down and seemed to understand that I appreciated and understood stories. Within days, I could read and was on my way.

There was no preparation for school whatsoever, before you got there. Mothers weren't allowed inside the lych gate at the entrance. My mother, being a frugal soul from the north, felt that there was no point in buying a uniform to fit a child aged five, as I would so rapidly grow out of it, so she bought an entire uniform for me in size 8 – so I'd get a good three years' worth of wear out of it. As I was always a very small child, the school blazer was tucked back up my arms so much that my arms stuck out almost at right angles to my body. The school hat and shoes were also far too large, and I thought this was a very odd thing, that you had to go to school in clothes that were clearly too big for you. My shoes were like flippers.

My first day at school was untraumatic until two things went wrong: the first was when a teacher came up to us and retrieved me from my mother and said, 'It's okay, pick her up at 3.30, I'm sure she won't cry,' whereupon I burst into tears, thinking, for the first time, 'Maybe my mother isn't coming back'. Then we all sat down at round tables with little round-backed infants chairs, like three-legged milking stools. Then the teacher launched abruptly into the alphabet. She asked who knew how to spell their name. I knew how to spell mine, because it was only four letters, but it wasn't until that moment that I realised that my name was odd. In those days, 'Lisa' was exotic. The whole class was full of Susans, Jeans, Peters, Johns and Gillians, with some Sarahs. Essentially, a sea of Susans. Some children asked me where my name had come from, and I answered, 'My mother'.

I remember a lot of fun, a lot of cutting out and drawing and colouring in and pasting, which was my idea of heaven. Then afternoon sleep time, when we all had to put our heads on our desks round about 2 p.m., and the blinds were drawn, and then came that incredibly delicious drowsiness you felt. It was as though you were in a giant pram, with the gentle snuffling of other children around you and the teacher looking after you. It felt so safe and secure.

Our first teacher reassured us that there was nothing to this reading and writing lark, it was as easy as knitting. Well. I completely panicked, because I couldn't knit. So when I got home that afternoon I insisted my mother teach me how to knit quickly, because this was going to be the key to literacy.

On St David's Day in my Welsh village, we wore full national costume to school. Our mothers stayed up half the night making little black Welsh hats, complete with white lace frills (often made from paper doilies) to frame your face. The hats were made from cardboard which was painted either with black paint or with black shoe polish. They were worn with shawls and pinafores. You had to take your best doll, which could be tricky, as they were often enormous – almost as big as we were – and very awkward to carry about!

Our desks in Infants had holes for inkwells, but of course we weren't allowed to use pens so young, so the holes stayed empty. My aim in life was to be big enough to have ink in my inkwell.

I hated Infants School because it seemed to me to be very strict, and I was frightened of all the teachers. I felt extremely victimised because each classroom had a Wendy house, with cups and saucers inside, and there were certain cloths you used to wipe these cups and saucers, and others you used to clean the floor. One girl went to the teacher and claimed that I'd cleaned the floor with the cloth used to wipe the dishes, and I had to stay in over playtime. And it was all lies. I couldn't believe it had happened to me. It still rankles, hundreds of years later.

To get to our Infants' School, we had to walk through a farmyard. It sounds as though we come from the nineteenth century rather than this one, because there was a duck pond and cart-horses, and hens. The farmer's daughter would come to our house, selling eggs.

PRIMARY SCHOOL
Primary schools in the 1950s were only just emerging from the Victorian influence. We didn't exactly have slates and backboards, but discipline was still very strict. We were expected to sit up straight and keep our mouths shut except when asked a question. We said the Lord's Prayer every morning. We marched in crocodile formation, holding hands. Teachers were gods, just like parents, and children who dared to misbehave were given a smack with the ruler or sent to the head for further punishment.

I remember my primary school teacher frothing at the mouth about boys wearing jeans. (No girl in the early fifties would have dreamed of wearing such things, and only a very few boys did.) The teacher said some parents claimed jeans kept legs clean. 'Nothing,' she thundered, 'can keep legs clean other than soap and water.'

I was very proud of my satchel, which was brown leather with two buckles. My mother had to put extra notches in the straps because I was so small that if she hadn't it would have trailed along the ground behind me.

There was a game played in the schoolyard of my primary school, mostly by boys against girls, but not exclusively. You only got caught once. Another kid would come up to you with an outspread palm, with a bunched fist at the back of it. 'Smell cheese,' they'd say, encouragingly, innocently. You'd thrust your face forward to sniff – and Pow! Your nose would be punched hard by the suddenly propelled fist.

Some of the male teachers we had were far from gentle. Everyone was scared of them. They'd whack kids at the drop of a hat, they'd bang people's heads together, dangerous stuff like that. The sort of behaviour that they'd be taken to court for today. No one complained.

The element of fear was always there. We had the cane, at our primary school. I managed to get it once — well, it wasn't a cane, it was a walking stick. It was a really bad thing to happen, you got your name put in a crimes book and everything. I was only about seven or eight. I pushed a guy over a wall to get a ball and there was an Alsatian dog on the other side which bit him on the bum. Well, he'd kicked my football over the fence and we couldn't play on without it.

I remember the beanbag as being a very important piece of equipment at my primary school. We used beanbags for all kinds of things, from sport to art, and they always seemed so friendly – just the right size to be clutched in a child-sized hand, just the right weight to be thrown, with a lovely fluid feeling when you squeezed them.

I was so advanced as a reader when I went to primary school that I used to have to spend my lunch hours (or dinnertimes, as we called them) teaching those kids who couldn't read. Some of them had nits, and I dreaded getting close to them. I resented this bitterly at the time, and in retrospect I still do.

Painting was my favourite. The joy was to do it as neatly and as beautifully as possible, with your tin palette of water colours. Or drawing with Lakeland colour pencils. I could colour in for hours and hours and hours. I thought painting by numbers was great. And you never, ever went outside the lines.

Nits were such a problem, even with kids who had really short hair. I remember sitting in front of one boy watching a louse make its way up his head. I avoided sitting near him after that, but I got nits anyway. I didn't realise that all the kids in my class had them.

One teacher at our primary school would wait until a pupil was absorbed in something of their own rather than listening to her. Then she'd make elaborate shushing gestures at the rest of the class, tiptoe up to the felon and THUMP the poor kid hard in the back. It's a wonder there weren't any heart attacks, the assaults were so sudden and so violent.

There were huge families of children at our school, really poor children with no shoes and things like that. We'd have a Christmas party, and every child had to take something to eat. I'd take a nice tin with fairy cakes in it; some children used to bring jam sandwiches.

Kids were caned a lot at our school, but I wasn't because I was middle class and obedient. Only the poor kids and the cheeky kids got caned, or at the very least had their hands strapped with a ruler.

Commonwealth Day was a big thing. All the children had to get dressed up as a member of a commonwealth country. All the children at the school were white, so the boy chosen to be a black boy had to have black stuff smeared all over his face. He had a hole in his trousers, where his bottom showed, and we had to put black stuff there as well.

The girls sometimes used to get pulled through the boys' toilets, which was all right except for the smell. Even at eight or nine, there was a terrible smell of blokes. The toilets had no roofs so the toilet paper was kept in the classrooms. If you wanted to go to the toilet during class, you had to put your hand up to ask permission, of course – but you also had to go to the front of the class and specify how many sheets of toilet paper you needed, that is, whether you were going to do big or small jobs. Then you'd run across the playground clutching your paper.

There were 'fever toilets' at my school. There was a row of six toilets, and the first two were known as 'fever toilets' – if you used them, you'd get a fever. We all knew this. So they were never, ever used. It created quite a problem with queuing at the remaining four.

We all played in the air-raid shelters at the back of the school, in the playing field. They were like grassed-over cellars.

BAIRNS-WEAR

school knitwear

Keen on his lessons he may be, but he's full of mischief, too. Never mind! Mother dresses him in the right woollies for work or play— Bairns-Wear school knitwear. She knows they wash like a dream and wear almost forever. Regulation styles and colours for girls and boys of all ages.

I remember so many puddles appearing on the floor at the feet of embarrassed and frightened children. Because you had to ask permission to leave the room to go to the toilet, and sometimes that permission was not granted.

had to sit wherever they could find a space on another kid's desk.

There were 48 kids in my class, and we were divided into four teams of 12. I was in the red team, St George's, and we sat in rows. I was leader, and had a little red badge. We'd have exams twice a term, and you had to stand in front of the class in order of how well you'd done. It was very competitive.

One day we all went out on the school field to play rounders, and everybody seemed to know how to play. Except I didn't. How did the others know? I had no idea what to do. I flung the bat at the ball and ran as hard as I could.

We always had big classes. It was only later that you realised that having 40 kids in a classroom was probably not all that good an idea. Some were just left behind, or neglected. I remember primary school as being really busy – maybe because there were so many kids in each class.

The wall around our school playground was topped with iron railings, but they'd been commissioned for the war effort to make munitions, so in the early fifties they were just stubs. And I thought that was normal, that was what iron railings looked like: inch-high points sticking out of stone.

We had work books to work through, and I was very competitive about getting through them. There were 40-odd of us in our class. We had a mix of whole-class and informal group teaching, and I remember the whole feel was one of teaching excellence. I remember their names and characters, and feel that they're friends still.

I used to get into trouble all the time because I wrote with my left hand, and my writing sloped the wrong way. My hand was slapped with a ruler more than once, for that. I don't know how they got away with it, really.

Our reports were very carefully written, and we always got marks out of 10 for every subject. It was a very structured, orderly way of learning.

We always had a weekly spelling test, and I've never forgotten any of the words I learnt in those tests.

I remember making an elaborate sewing bag cum apron, with a folded-up bit which you put all your bits and pieces in and then you tied it around your waist. It had embroidered patterns all over it.

There were 53 in my class, but only 50 desks. We were seated at the desks in order of accomplishment, but the last three in the class

We seemed to spend an awful lot of time doing really useless things, like embroidering tray cloths or making peg bags or long cylinders to keep spills in.

P.E. classes were held in conjunction with the programme on the radio. There was a huge radio on the stage, and you'd exercise in time with things played on it, such as 'Row, row, row your boat'. We'd all sit there on the floor, energetically pretending to row.

We used to do country dancing in a big way, enter competitions. Morris dancing. There were competitions all over the country, and once a year we'd have a big inter-school country dancing competition at Alexandra Palace.

Our school band had things like clappers, and triangles, and one tinny drum. We weren't encouraged to learn a real musical instrument at all.

Why did we collect jam jars? For a very long time, we were told to collect empty jam jars, wash them and take them to school. We never asked why, of course.

We had to keep scrapbooks on the Royal Family for school projects. I kept one on Lady Mountbatten – now why on earth would I do that?

So much of our news reporting seemed to consist of stories about the Royal Family, especially Prince Charles and Princess Anne. We followed their activities as avidly as any tabloid reader follows the Royal Family's antics today.

The last couple of weeks of the first term of each year were devoted to Christmas preparations. The school Nativity Play, singing carols, making decorations for your classroom, making cards. The festive sense was huge. Before Easter, too, and Lent: Pancake Day, Ash Wednesday. Empire Day.

I remember feeling very confused at school, I felt at a disadvantage because I didn't know what was going on, and why. I had a lot of problems in that respect. People used to talk about getting the scholarship, and I thought they meant you got a ship, in a bottle. I believed that until I was quite old.

When I got into the final year of primary school I knew that the most important thing in the world was to pass the eleven-plus. Then, even when you'd passed, the next most important thing was choosing the right school and getting into it. I can remember taking the envelope up to my parents, who were in bed. And I'd passed.

We used to be called 'grammar snobs' by the kids who hadn't passed the eleven-plus. In a way, it was more of a stigma to have passed than not, in my Welsh village.

I remember doing the eleven-plus for three Saturday mornings running, in the local high school. We had an English test one Saturday, a maths test the next week, then an IQ test. I'd never done an IQ test before, so I guessed most of it, not realising that this could have affected the rest of my life.

My Fifties

BOB AYLING (B. 1946)
I remember growing up in the leafy Surrey suburbs: short trousers; girls with plaits; Montessori school equipment; copperplate handwriting; the shadow of war stories from my parents; lots of bicycling (which was safe then); working in my father's grocery shop in the holidays and learning to count change in pounds, shillings and pence, which improved my mental arithmetic.

Sunday School

These are the recollections of Church of England children, because that was the prevailing religion of the fifties. We were possibly the last generation to attend church regularly.

My sister and I went to Sunday school for years, mainly to collect the pictures they gave you for good attendance. Then for some reason we rebelled and decided we'd play truant, playing in the fields near us during the time we were supposed to be in church. But we couldn't bring ourselves to spend the collection money our mother gave us, so we'd throw the lot into the field behind our house when we were sure no one was looking. There must have been a fortune scattered around there in the end.

I got a cup for never missing a day of Sunday school for a year. I used to go with my father to this chapel on Sunday afternoon, they'd have a musical do, a mixture of prayer and music. I can remember them playing 'Lilac Time', then a fire and brimstone preacher would bang on. Very odd.

You'd get a picture, a stamp, every week for attending, and you could stick them in an album. That was the best thing about going. The pictures were of Christ on the Cross, or somebody going into a burning bush. If you filled the album, you got a Sunday School prize. You did your best to get as many stamps as possible.

My father grew up in a strongly Methodist working class family, and my mother came from a more liberal Church of England family. So I ended up having to go to church three

times on Sundays. But I have really happy memories of it. I was involved in plays and performance and acting there. The first time I ever appeared on stage, I must have been about three, was singing 'Over the Rainbow' at Sunday School. Going to church was what you did. You had to put your best clothes on and sit there in this draughty ancient Gothic building.

We weren't allowed to play out in the front garden or the back garden on Sundays. You could go outside, but you weren't allowed to make a noise. And we weren't even chapel people.

I didn't get christened until quite late. I remember the day I was christened, in white clothes almost like Confirmation clothes, and I had the little white gloves, the little white dress, the little white shoes and the little white socks. I desperately wanted a pair of frilly socks, but my mother thought they were common so that was that. I asked her why I was being christened, because I knew my name, and surely everybody else knew it, including God. But of course I had to go through with it, and I was too small to reach the font and too large to be held in someone's arms, so they put me on a hassock and the priest made the sign of the cross on me, plus two circles. I said in a very loud voice, 'Why has he written Oxo on my forehead?'

I remember the rituals: Christmas, Easter, harvest festivals. Immensely cosy rituals, with wonderful hymns. There was a big harvest supper every year in the village in the Memorial Hall. That was a major celebration.

The harvest festival at our church was a bit embarrassing, really, because I think the original idea was to take some of your own produce in to be distributed to the poor and needy, to give thanks for the bountiful harvest on your own land. And of course we all lived in a town and had tiny gardens and were lucky if our parents grew a couple of tomatoes in a greenhouse. So we ended up taking bought stuff, some of it in tins, in the end, and it all got a bit silly. There were always loaves of bread at the front of the display. I reckon the vicar got most of it.

'Walking Day' was a procession of witness for the church: you witnessed that you were a believer, and you carried banners with streamers. You had to wear a posh frock to carry a banner, which proclaimed things like 'God is Love'. All the girls on any one banner had to have dresses made of the same material, so we'd go into town together and get flocked nylon, which you only ever wore on Walking Day. You wouldn't dream of ever wearing it again. But the good thing was that you could go up to people on Walking Day and smile nicely and introduce yourself, and they'd be obliged to give you threepence. Threepence!

CHRIS WOODHEAD *My Fifties*
(HM CHIEF INSPECTOR OF SCHOOLS B. 1946)

I remember standing at the end of our road spotting car numbers – no more than a couple of cars every ten minutes – now, of course, a constant stream.
I also remember the horse-drawn milk floats, the trolley buses and the fog, and men in bowler hats.
The coach ride to Weston-super-Mare for summer holidays took forever on the A4. If I wasn't sick before the coffee stop at Maidenhead, I knew I'd be alright.
As for school, I recall the rows of desks, the fairly competitive classroom ethos, the horror and incompetence I felt when confronted by compulsory needlework.

PART 2
Fun and games galore

What we played with

It's true that we had far fewer toys than children do these days. If you got a handful of presents each birthday and Christmas, you were doing well. So we did have to rely more on our imagination, on found objects, and on fantasy and make-believe.

Toys

The rigid divide between girls' toys and boys' toys was alive and well in the fifties. But, so soon after the war, we were lucky to have toys and a safe environment to play with them in.

JUNE 1956

VOL. XLI No.

MECCANO
MAGAZINE

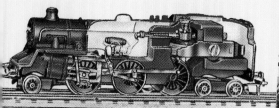

My sister and I had lots of peg dolls. It seems so sad and austere now, to have dolls made out of wooden clothes pegs, but they were just as interesting and enjoyable to us as more elaborate dolls.

My mother once made me a doll out of some lengths of black wool tied together at the top. She was no more than a pompom with a sewn-on face, really, but I called her Dot and loved her dearly.

Now, there's everything to assist imagination. But in those days we had to be imaginative ourselves. Things like Meccano sets – they're plastic now, but any lad who had a Meccano set in the fifties knew about tensions; knew how tight to do something up; had that feel already. Men and their Morris 1000s!

All the boys in our neighbourhood had train sets. I'd beg and plead to play with them, and had wonderful afternoons when permission was grudgingly granted. But as a girl I had no chance of ever getting one of my own. This was understood implicitly – it never even occurred to me to ask for one. But then, it wasn't the trains that interested me, it was the villages and towns and countryside the train sets travelled through.

We all had these French knitting machines, which were nothing more than a hollow wooden tube, a bit like a cotton reel, with four or five wire hoops bent into the top. You twisted the wool around each one in turn. What came out the other end was an endless thin sausage of knitted wool, and the really hard part was figuring out what on earth to do with it.

I still have my autograph book from 1955. I'm the proud owner of the signatures of Steve (The Bachelors), Mike Preston, Bruce Welch, Hank Marvin, Wee Willie Harris and Jimmy Young (twice).

I was given dolls, but because I had a brother and male cousins they never lasted long. Especially the one with the china head. I loved that doll, but it didn't last a minute. The only durable doll I had, the only one to survive my male siblings, was a rag doll.

My biggest thrill was on my third birthday, receiving my pedal car. I was so delighted; it was that moment, that joy, that sticks in my mind more than anything from my childhood.

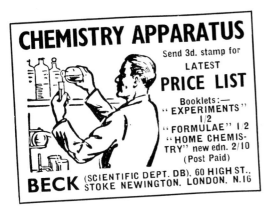
Children could buy the most amazing chemicals over the counter then. I used to get iodine from the chemist's and ammonia from the hardware shop and mix them together. This resulted in an unstable ball that was in effect a home-made bomb, which would go off unexpectedly (a touch from a feather duster would be enough to set it off) and at length – pop, pop, pop, pop. I can't remember the chemical formula because of course all my chemistry books were destroyed in one final attempt to control the substance. I also used to buy hydrochloric acid.

I still have my Triang pile-driver, and people can't stop playing with it. It's wooden, and you push the bits of wood in and they whoosh out. It's fifty years old now, but I don't think it was new even when I was given it. Lots of toys then were hand-me-downs.

My brother and I used to play shops with the old ration books, once they weren't needed any more.

My father made a lot of my toys. I had a wonderful train made out of paint tins that you could sit on. He also made me a farm out of corrugated paper and mirrors.

Dad got me a balsa-wood kit to make a glider. You could buy a tiny little jet motor, called a Jet-X, I think, to put in it – a little cylinder with a sort of combustible tablet to put inside. You put a wick in one side, screwed the end in, and it gave a sort of jet propulsion for a couple of minutes.

I had a tricycle that I rode to my grandparents' house – I had to cross the main Bristol road. Then they moved, and I had to ride it over a mile to their new place. No one thought it dangerous, or odd. It was assumed that everyone would look out for children.

that used to secure fencing wire to posts. Hit me right in the eye. He also fired a fire extinguisher in my face once, because it looked like a gun. I was blinded for about half an hour, and had to have drops in my eyes for weeks afterwards.

My father had a childless brother, Uncle Dick, who made me my dolls' house. I can still remember the little latch at the side. He wallpapered it for me, and painted it, and made every single piece of furniture in it. It was modelled on a Nottingham terrace house. He made toys for me in his shed: little boxes to put things in.

Everybody seemed to have a little farm, with miniature animals. They were really popular. I used to save all my pocket money to buy plastic cows – called Bluebell and Daisy – and horses (the carthorse was always called Dobbin) and ducks. I don't ever remember buying a sheep, or a goat.

In the years after the war, guns were all the rage. Guns and crossbows; weapons in general. My friend made a crossbow once and nearly took my eye out. It was a crossbow that fired those staple nails

DINKY TOYS

No. 716
Westland-Sikorsky Helicopter
Length overall 3¼ in. 2/6

No. 735
Gloster Javelin Delta Wing Fighter
Wing Span 3¼ in. 2/6

No. 131
Cadillac Eldorado Tourer
Length 4½ in. 4/6

No. 106
Austin Atlantic Convertible
Length 3¾ in. 3/3

No. 455
Trojan 15-cwt. Van
'BROOKE BOND TEA'
Length 3¼ in. 2/9

No. 443
Tanker 'NATIONAL BENZOLE'
Length 4¾ in. 2/11

No. 670
Armoured Car
Length 2¼ in. 3/3

No. 621
3-ton Army Wagon
Length 4½ in. 5/3

No. 164
Vauxhall Cresta Saloon
Length 3½ in. 3/-

No. 190
Caravan
Length 4¾ in. (including towbar) 3/11

MADE IN ENGLAND BY MECCANO LTD., BINNS ROAD, LIVERPOOL 13

Just like the real thing!

Airfix kits are not just models — they're exact *replicas*, each series to a constant scale.

Airfix 1/72nd scale Lancaster bomber. 17" wing span. 7/6d.

Aircraft (*all to the same 1/72nd scale*), 00 gauge railway accessories, vintage cars, historical ships. Airfix value is *unbeatable!*

Nearly 100 kits from 2/- to 7/6d.

We had lots of jigsaws. The Cinderella Pantomime Jigsaw was always done at Christmas, then it was covered by the tablecloth to keep it from being scattered. We had several featuring armadas and sailing ships – to this day, I look up at certain cloud formations tinged with pink and shout, 'It's a jigsaw sky!' Sea and sky.

The main board game was Monopoly. Nearly everyone seemed to have that. And Ludo, and Snakes and Ladders.

I got a pedal car, which was very unusual for a girl. It was maroon, with a white steering wheel. Living on the side of a hill, there were very few places I could drive it. There was a crazy paving path leading from the back of the house to the shed, so I drove my car down the stairs and along this path, then out into the road like Toad of Toad Hall. I lost control halfway down the hill and cannoned into the local policeman. He took me home, I was smacked and the car was impounded. I still loved it, though.

We didn't have lots of toys compared with children now. But my wish-list always had board games on it – I especially liked the classics like Chinese Chequers, Tiddly Winks and Ludo – and I would spend literally hours playing with them. I suppose my parents thought it was a good way to keep me quiet. But I've never forgotten how pretty they were, the sound of the dice in the cups and the slippery feel of the counters. The colours and patterns have always stayed in my memory.

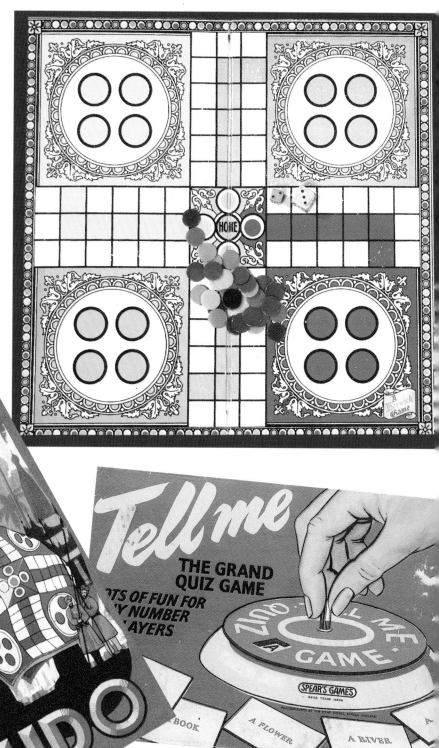

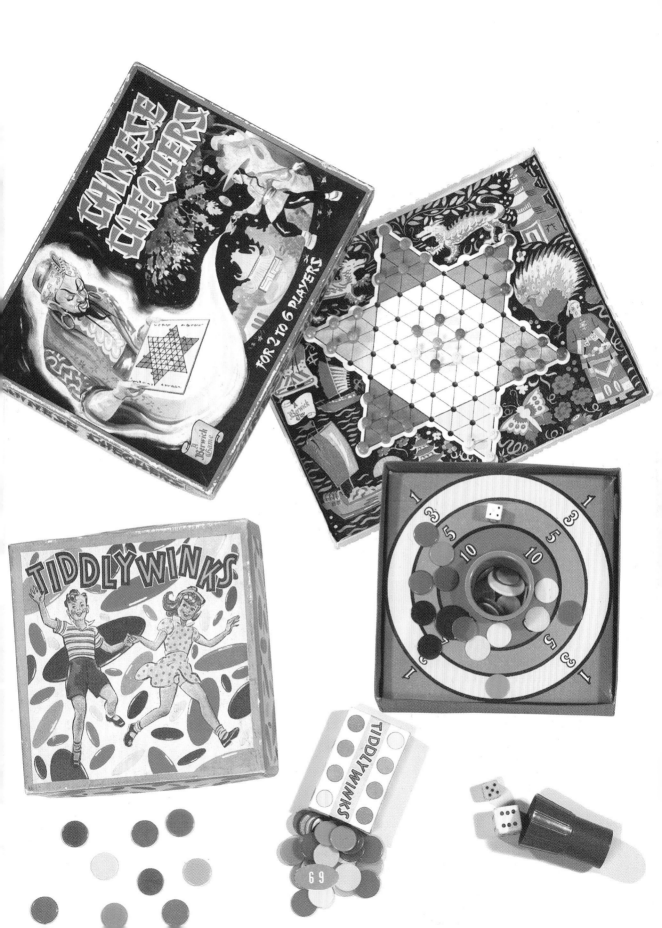

Neighbourhood games and sports

With little traffic to interrupt us, most of us played out on the streets of our neighbourhood if there wasn't a local park. We have a shared memory of childhood spent predominantly outdoors, despite the notorious British weather.

No street was without its hopscotch lines chalked on the pavement. It was mostly a girls' game, like skipping; I don't remember any of the boys ever playing.

Scraps were a huge craze. We'd spend hours, days even, swapping scraps. We bought the scraps, then we swapped them. The favourites were very Victorian – women in crinolines, girls with violets, cherubs, baskets of flowers. To look at them now, they seem to belong to the nineteenth century, not the 1950s. But we loved them. They're still around, of course, but adults use them now for decoupage.

LESLEY O'MARA
(B. 1954)

My Fifties

I remember the highlight of my preschool days was Andy Pandy. Of course, there were no mother and toddler singalong or baby gyms in those days! The little boy from next door used to come in and watch it and I remember thinking how babyish he was because he used to cry when the theme music started to indicate that it was over for the day.

Bill and Ben was nearly as good. I particularly liked WEEED but I bought a video of it a few years ago when my children were small and they thought I was mad – couldn't see the point of it all! Shame the children have changed so much.

We played a lot of juggling games with balls, or 'stotting' them against a wall. I remember one rhyme for two balls went:
Shirley Eaton, Shirley Eaton
She's a star – S-T-A-R!
Other rhymes were:
'Mademoiselle from Armentieres
Parlez-vous?'
and
'House to let
Apply within . . .'
and
'I'm a little Dutch girl
Dressed in blue . . .'
and
'Jelly on a plate, jelly on a plate
Wibbly wobbly wibbly wobbly
Jelly on a plate.'

The older girls, the fourteen-year-olds, were brilliant at skipping. We used to use the washing line in the street, and it was enormous. Two strong lads would hold the line, one at each end, and we'd all chant *Salt, Vinegar, Mustard . . . PEPPER!* and the boys would swing this huge rope, starting slowly on salt and going as fast as they could on pepper. Only the older girls could handle that. We'd play along the side of the road. If a car came someone would shout 'Car!', but it didn't happen often enough to seriously disturb the game.

A whole lot of us would play 'What time is it, Mr Wolf?' out on the street. You had to creep up on 'Mr Wolf' by taking the number of steps he called out as the time – three o'clock would mean three steps, and so on – but the idea was to cheat and tag him before he could tag you.

I seemed to spend half my life standing on my head against a wall, or doing handstands.

Cowboys and Indians were really popular – although I didn't know anyone who had an Indian outfit, we were all cowboys. The whole of the local village would play; the game would go on for days. Every so often you had to die, and lie there on the ground. Then you'd get fed up with that, and join in again. We all had guns, but you'd always run out of caps and have to go 'Pow, pow!' It was a fabulous game, although there was no rhyme or reason to it, none at all.

Every winter the whole gang would sledge down a steep neighbourhood street on a variety of home-made and bought sledges. It's a wonder there weren't more accidents, but about the worst that happened was some of us – me included – going home crying with the cold after an hour or so. I'd have to practically thrust my hands into the fire to thaw them out after making snowballs.

One thing we did in a big way was make trolleys, soap-boxes, particularly if you lived in a hilly area. It was all to do with the design of prams. They had two big wheels and an axle, and you could take the wheels off and sign an IOU to your friend for 2s/6d to get his axle. Then you could make your own soap box with wood, and put a brake on, and a steering wheel. I remember one I made, an eight-wheeler, which had two-axle steering, and four of us could sit on it and shoot down a hill. Another was like an armoured car: a box, essentially, on top of a trolley, and you'd go along steering it and have a little slit to look out of, and all the other children would throw all these bricks at you, so it'd be bang bang bang down the hill. You couldn't possibly do that today because it's so dangerous.

Life was just a total game, we played games non-stop. Things like eating or sleeping or going shopping or having your hair cut were just interruptions to having a good time, playing cricket or football.

My Fifties

LORD (MAURICE) SAATCHI (B. 1946)
I have no memories of childhood. Life on earth began at the age of 11, getting off the 210 bus at the stop outside our new house in Highgate, after my first day at my new school. Apart from knowing the street where I lived in Hampstead, what happened for the preceding 11 years is a blank. Psychiatrists would have a field day...

There were four other boys my age in our street, so we had a proper gang. We spent most of our time outdoors, playing football, cricket, anything involving a ball. We never played with girls.

There was a wood just up the road, where we had our favourite tree – the old oak tree. If I couldn't find any of my friends, or they weren't home, I'd just go up to the old oak tree and there'd be someone there. We climbed it, swung from it, built platforms and houses in it. It was like our headquarters. As we grew older we reached higher and higher branches.

We played this game called Kick the Can. It was like Hide and Seek, except it featured a can you had to get back to unseen, and kick it to win.

I used to pinch golf balls from the local course and sell them at a shop in town. I stole Cliff Michelmore's golf ball once. He was a terrible golfer and his balls always landed in the rough. It was my prize possession for ages.

We didn't have any swimming lessons at school. You left primary school at 11 or 12 unable to even swim. We taught ourselves to swim at the local pool – you just learned by hammering away at the water for a while in the deep end. If you didn't swim you would drown, so that's how you learned.

Hobbies

Hobbies were part of post-war childhood. You were expected to have a hobby, by your school, your parents and even by your friends. It was part and parcel of the 'Devil makes work for idle hands' philosophy that ruled how children's time was spent.

Everyone in the world had to have a hobby in those days. I could never understand the attraction of stamp collecting, but we did it, simply because everybody did. If I had to fill in a CV form today, I'd probably put 'Stamp collecting' under 'Hobbies or Interests'.

We used to spend our pocket money on little packets of stamps from the Post Office. You could get a large packet of mixed stamps, which were mostly rubbish, or small packets of more select stamps.

We (and by we I mean boys) all used to collect birds' eggs. It was part of climbing trees and falling off.
The impact on nature was not that great, I hope. We only ever took one egg from each nest. I used to stick pins in moths and butterflies, too. But they all rot, eventually.

We used to go to tap dancing classes in a big hall over the Co-op. We'd dance to 'Papa Picolino'. I had little red tap shoes.

We were each given our own small patch of the garden to cultivate and tend. I remember the joy of growing love-in-a-mist, marigolds and forget-me-nots. I still try to grow those flowers, and other old-fashioned species from our garden then, such as hollyhocks, foxgloves and wallflowers.

The whole family played cards every Sunday afternoon. Knockout Whist, a form of rummy, and Newmarket with matches. Occasionally the adults would bet with money and let us kids win. A halfpenny each, or something.

I used to collect train and bus numbers, and I'd save up my pocket money to buy the books that had the numbers in them that you crossed out when you spotted them. An anorak from way back.

We belonged to the 'I Spy' books. You could join the club, and you got sent badges and things.

I-SPY SPORT 6ᴰ
NEWS CHRONICLE I-SPY Nº 19

Social life

Social life in the fifties, especially for children, was a rare creature, seldom seen. But what we did have was a very strong sense of family, and an equally strong sense of community, of neighbourhood.

The highlight of my social life when I was about eight or nine was visiting my friend's house for tea. She lived a few houses up the road, but it was very exciting to go there and have banana sandwiches, and sometimes her mother would get us those cut-out cardboard dolls with paper clothes and little flaps to keep them on. Bliss!

Our parents belonged to various clubs – the Round Table and the Ladies' Circle were the main ones – and they seemed to be forever going out to glamorous events such as Fancy Dress Balls, which involved endless preparations and costumes and our cousins coming to babysit. Our mother would always be very excited on the day, and when she finally appeared in the living room wearing her ball gown, or costume, or whatever, with her hair done in sausage rolls and wafting trails of Chanel No 5 or Evening in Paris, it was as though we'd been visited by an apparition from Hollywood or New York. They once went to see a local production of *Call me Madam*, and for months afterwards they'd burst into 'There's No Business Like Show Business', dancing around the kitchen flourishing imaginary top hats and canes.

We used to love going to the neighbourhood Beetle Drives. 'Beetle' was a dice game where you had to draw the outline of a beetle on a sheet of paper by filling in the details – body, head, feelers, legs, eyes – according to the numbers you threw with the dice. The first on each table to complete the beetle won that round, then all the round winners would compete for the grand final. Beetle Drives were so exciting.

I remember learning to dance and going to neighbourhood dances in scout halls, austere places with chairs lined around the walls. We danced the Valeta, and the Dashing White Sergeant, and the Gay Gordons. They were good fun.

No one ever came to our house except relatives, and we never went out except to visit relatives. The only house I ever ate at, apart from our own, was my grandfather's. I ate there every Friday, before Cubs. I'd have bacon and egg.

Eating out was virtually unheard of in fifties suburbia. Once in a blue moon our mother would take us to a local department store cafeteria for tea; she and her friends would sit sipping tea and watching the mannequins – as they were then called – modelling the latest fashions.

I have a strong memory of the fact that in the mid-fifties, families would go for walks together in the evenings. These were pre-television days, so there were no distractions, and the big

social occasion of the day for us was the evening walk. The number of people outside in the evenings was phenomenal, and the world had a far friendlier feel. I remember just walking around, seeing so many people, talking at corners and so on. Cars and TV were the start of the social isolation of many neighbourhoods.

My parents had some friends we used to visit occasionally, and I can remember thinking them so exotic, so strange, because they were a married couple but they had no children. They were the only such people I ever met as a child.

What we joined

Joining things – societies, charity organisations, quasi-military set-ups – was also part and parcel of growing up in the fifties. Few of us escaped the net entirely.

I was a member of the Boys Brigade, which had a more military bearing than the Boy Scouts. It was the forerunner of the Cadet Corps, for boys round the age of seven to eleven. We went on camps, marched around, and did things like first aid, working with wood. It was fun. We went on one huge expedition to Exeter, which was an early insight into how friction can occur because the guy in charge fell out with the officer and stormed off in a huff. I still have my hats and badges.

My mother was a Brown Owl, so I joined and got all my badges. I remember polishing those bloody badges! She was really strict about it. By the time of the Guides, I'd lost interest. I remember the Jamborees at Wolverhampton. We all sang, and had to dance up this middle aisle towards Princess Margaret. And there were loads of competitions, including Greek dancing, which everyone did then, very expressively.

I joined the Brownies but I was sacked because I stole the subs money to spend on sweeties. I couldn't see the point of Brownies anyway, all that dib dib dib stuff. I could never learn to tie the tie, so I'd pull it over my head – but Brown Owl would check to see if it was freshly tied each week. This was another tyranny I could do without. I think I was an elf, or a fairy, or a sprite. I did quite like the fancy dress element, though: Brownie parties, where I went as a carrot.

We belonged to Enid Blyton's Busy Bees, which meant that you raised money for the PDSA, essentially. We read about each other's exploits in *The Enid Blyton Magazine* – subtitled 'The Only Magazine I Write', which made Pa laugh. On page 2, there was always a letter from Enid Blyton, from 'Green Hedges, Beaconsfield, Bucks', telling us about her children.

GIRL ADVENTURERS

This was a club that readers of *Girl* could join, provided they filled in one of the coupons in the magazine and sent it in with a postal order for one shilling and sixpence. In return they would receive a club badge – a delightful brooch of a girl's head in gilt, with the words 'Girl Adventurers' underneath it – and a membership card which listed the club rules:

'RULES

1. GIRL ADVENTURERS will:

a) Enjoy life in a way that helps others to enjoy life too. They will not enjoy themselves at the expense of others.

b) Strive to develop themselves in body, mind and spirit. They will feel it is their duty to make the best of themselves.

c) Work for the good of all around them.

d) Be thoughtful for the needs and feelings of other people.

e) Set an example of kindness to animals.

f) Give up part of their own time every day in order to help others.

2. The GIRL ADVENTURERS exist:

a) To promote the ideals of living outlined in the rules.

b) For comradeship between all who accept the rules given above.

c) To organise meetings and expeditions for members.'

Club activities included Hobbies Advice Bureau, Pen Pals Group and Holidays:

'During 1955 in cooperation with the Youth Hostel Association we were able to organise our Walking and Cycling tours. These proved to be even more successful than the 1954 series. One of the greatest concessions for club members is our *GIRL* Ballet Scholarship scheme run in association with the Royal Academy of Dancing and the Sadler's Wells School, and many Adventurers took advantage of it last year. They also took part in the *EAGLE/GIRL* National Junior Table Tennis Tournament Competitions, Carol services, Circus visits and Christmas Parties. If you are not already a club member – join now!'

Party time celebrations

THE CORONATION
It was the biggest party of them all, a national celebration when whole communities got together to cheer the ascension to the throne of Queen Elizabeth II in 1953. It was also the first complete memory of past events many of us have.

Oh God, the coronation was such an exciting concept. That gold coach with all the horses, and the queen with her crown and ermine-edged robe, and the orb and sceptre – just like every fairy tale coming true. But the actual event was a bit boring. We crammed into a neighbour's house along with about a million other people to watch television for the first time. We took sandwiches and a Thermos flask. It went on and on and on, and there really wasn't much to hold the interest of a six-year-old. The two tortoises in the garden were much more interesting.

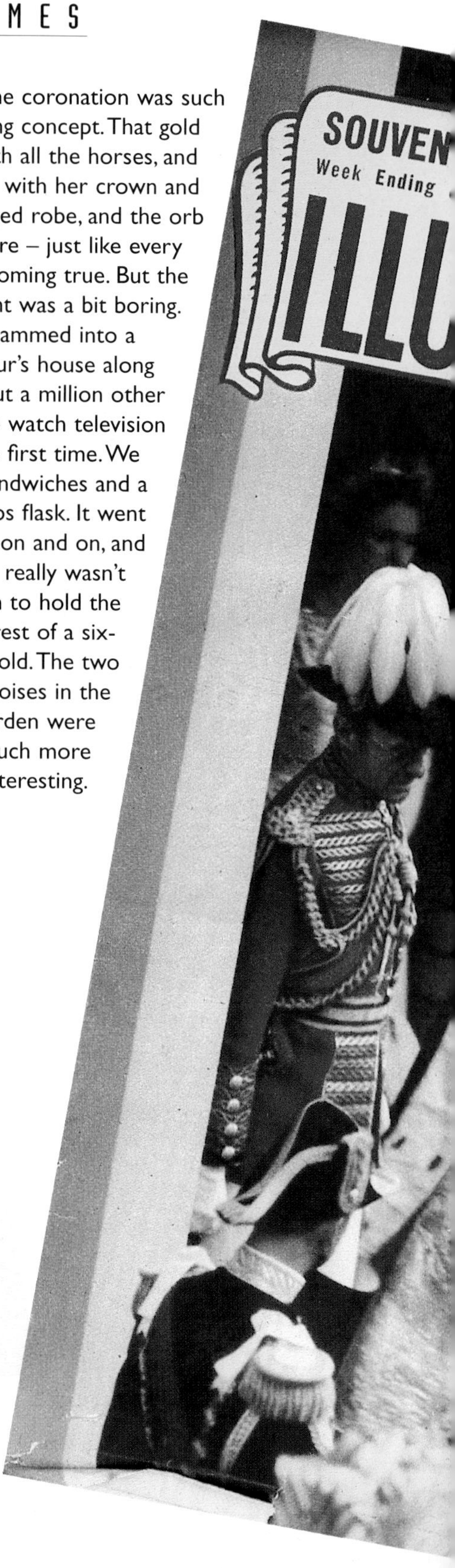

LOYAL GREETINGS
from the brewers of
DOUBLE DIAMOND
A DOUBLE DIAMOND WORKS WONDERS

SOUVEN
Week Ending
ILLU

UE 6d
953
THE CORONATION IN
WONDERFUL PICTURES
TRATED
With commentaries by
Sir Compton Mackenzie
H. V. Morton
Lord Kilbracken

The whole neighbourhood went to a party in a huge Nissen hut in the middle of the prefab estate. All the girls over a certain age were given a locket with a picture of the Queen and Prince Philip inside, but I wasn't old enough so all I got was a Coronation mug. My sister was given a locket, and I was so upset and made such a fuss that three lots of neighbours brought lockets to me over the next couple of days. I felt so ashamed, and had to hide the fact that I already had a locket from each of the last two.

I remember going into Swansea to watch the Coronation, and getting a little model of the coach and the double line of horses, and the gilt coming off the coach very shortly afterwards.

The people opposite us painted the boulders in their front garden with red, white and blue stripes, and put bunting out, so I knew it was going to be a really important event.

In school we had little kits and we made the coach and horses up out of pre-pressed cardboard, pop them up and glue them down. At the neighbourhood party, I got a Coronation mug, took it outside and dropped it.

My Dad bought me a sparkly cut-out model of the coach and horses and we assembled it into a 3-D model. It was the perfect size to fit in the fanlight of our front door. One house up the road had a model of the lion and the unicorn in the garden, it was there for years, a local landmark.

My Fifties

GENISTA McINTOSH
(B. 1946)
February 1952. I remember standing with my father in thick fog on Westminster Bridge, queueing to file past the coffin of King George VI as he lay in state. We don't have fogs like that any more.

FESTIVAL OF BRITAIN

The Labour government decreed that we should all start to enjoy ourselves and shake off the post-war gloom. A great festival exhibition celebrating the achievements of the country and Empire was built on an old bomb site on the south bank of the Thames, opposite Charing Cross. By the time it opened in 1951 the government had lost a snap election and was replaced by the Conservatives. The incoming party was less than enthusiastic about the festival, but the public flocked to it in their thousands. Britain loved the whole enterprise, from the 'Skylon' – that pointed upward like a futuristic rocket – to the 'Dome of Discovery'. It was extraordinarily ambitious but visually stunning.

I remember going to the Festival of Britain in 1951, and going on the Tree Walk. It was this really exciting elevated walkway through the trees in Battersea Park. Because I was so excited, I can see it now if I close my eyes.

My aunt and uncle took me to see the Skylon and as we walked across Hungerford Bridge I caught glimpses of it, along with the Dome through the iron work. It seemed to take forever to cross the footbridge that ran alongside the rail tracks and I thought surely no one can walk this far. The only exhibit I can remember is a man making cricket balls. I *was* only six.

I couldn't really work out what the Festival of Britain was for. An uncle who was rather better off than us actually went to London to see it – and he brought back the souvenir brochure. I remember staring at the pictures, trying to figure out what it all meant – what was the Skylon supposed to do? We did have

a huge street party though – all the kids wore their best clothes and sat at lines of tables which our parents had carried out into the street. They served amazing treats like pink blancmange in decorative moulds, ice cream; tinned fruit and Carnation milk – and we all tucked in for Britain.

During the Festival of Britain the whole village went into a frenzy of decorating the streets red white and blue. My father copied the festival symbol – a sort of shield with the head of Britannia on it – and stuck it proudly in the centre of the front railings. Britannia was flanked by red and white paper ribbons. As for my mother, she made hundreds of paper roses in red white and blue and attached them all over a large branch of a tree which she stuck in the front garden. It looked as if the tree had suddenly grown all these red white and blue roses. As for the rest of the village, it was the same story: houses absolutely groaning with red white and blue bunting.

The grown-ups celebrated the Festival of Britain in the most exciting ways. I remember they arranged a football match between the men and the women in the village. We were totally shocked to see our mothers dressed up in football kit – showing their pudgy little knees. But they loved it. They broke all the rules, kicked the ball wherever they wanted and threw the ref into the river when he tried to blow his whistle to call them offside. We children were laughing ourselves silly in the stands and cheering like mad!

BEL MOONEY (B. 1946) My Fifties

It is about 1954 and I am in my Nan's house in Liverpool, rummaging in the drawer in her fifties kitchen unit. It smells of food; there are paper bags spotted with grease, carefully smoothed and folded; bits of string and elastic bands wait for usefulness. I take out the stained ration books, and examine them curiously, before continuing the search for glue. She and I are going to make cushion covers from squares of saved black-out material. She cranks her hand-operated Singer energetically and creates the covers. Then it is my job to draw big petal and leaf shapes in coloured felt, cut them out, and stick them on. Once the old pads are stuffed in she shows me how to sew up the open sides – and there are the new cushions. I am as proud of them as of the new powder blue suit with velvet collar and pleated skirt my mother has made me. So busy we were – frugal and clever.

BIRTHDAYS

Fifties birthday parties closely resembled those of today, except that no one had such things as paid entertainers or jumping castles. But traditional food and games held sway: fairy bread, jelly, lemonade, 'Pass the Parcel', 'Musical Chairs', 'Blind Man's Buff', 'Pin the Tail on the Donkey'.

For my sixth birthday my mother organised for several of us to go to the Grotto, a local restaurant built into a cave at the bottom of a cliff – the height of sophistication. That was exciting enough, but the real treat was that she hired a taxi to take us there and back. It was the first time I'd ever been in a taxi, and the last for several years after that.

At one party I won a beautiful shiny bangle for reciting 'I know a man named Michael Finnegan, He had whiskers on his chinnegan . . .' and I was so proud of it I insisted on wearing it to bed that night. When I woke up in the morning my bed was full of bits of bangle.

We always had a birthday tea, with lots of jellies and pop, and bridge rolls, cut in half with fish paste or boiled eggs inside. And iced gems. We had proper party frocks, with rosebuds on them and sashes at the back.

I always had a big party in early October, I remember the weather as always being pretty good. I'd get some great presents, annuals like *Rupert Bear*. We had fizzy drinks and fairy cakes, the usual, with kids making themselves sick. But I never invited any girls.

All our birthday parties were identical, and they all had the same people at them, but on your birthday you were the special person, which made all the difference. Blowing out the candles was the most important ritual: blowing them out in one go made you a real man. None of these universal candles you get nowadays that come alight again after you've blown them out.

GUY FAWKES NIGHT
The smell of cordite in the sharp autumnal air remains a powerful memory for many of us. In the days before strict legislation, danger ruled okay.

One of the women in our street was a great organiser of street parties, and every year she'd buy a whole lot of fireworks for Bonfire Night. All the neighbourhood kids would gather firewood and we'd have a big bonfire in the vacant lot. One year, she'd spent a lot of money on fireworks for the whole gang as usual but one of us dropped a match into the box and they all went off together.

Kids could buy fireworks easily in those days – you could steal them pretty easily, too – big bangers and rockets. Once we opened up some fireworks and took this huge amount of gunpowder out to a tip, then put it into a big metal container to make a bomb. It didn't go off, so my pal went over to have a look. Just as he looked at it there was an almighty flash – I think he was lucky to survive, let alone be able to see.

Dad used to ceremoniously nail a Catherine Wheel to the old shed, just like about a million other fathers all over the country, and like them he'd watch it fizzle out half the time. I think that was part of the fun, the tradition of Bonfire Night: all these dads running around trying to be important, failing to make a good firework display.

EDWINA CURRIE
(B. 1946) *My Fifties*

I remember penny bars of chocolate – old pennies, that is, worthless today. Sweets and chocolate were rationed, so my grandmother used to save up her coupons and buy all her grandchildren these penny bars of Cadbury's. The contrast when a gift box came from relatives in Canada – boxes of M & Ms and Chiclets and as much as we could eat…

EASTER
Very much the poor cousin of Christmas, Easter was nevertheless celebrated with eggs, and cards, and, in many towns, parades.

There'd be an Easter Parade through the town every year, and you'd march along with your palm cross, and every year the weather would be foul. Women and children would struggle bravely along in their wispy finery, clutching their Easter bonnets against the howling gale and shivering in the icy rain. It became part of our family language: 'clutching your Easter bonnet' meant doing something outdoors in typical English weather.

We always got something new to wear for the Easter Parade. If you didn't, the crows would crap on you and you'd have bad luck. It was a well-known fact. So I usually got a new coat.

Our grandmothers would send us eggs every year, through the post, so of course they arrived in pieces. A lot of the chocolate had this fatty, vile taste, too, especially the cheap stuff from chain stores. It really had to be Cadbury's.

On Easter Sunday we'd have dyed boiled eggs. Ordinary eggs boiled in water with a bit of food colouring or dye in it.

ROYAL VISITS

The imminent arrival of a royal visitor sent town councils into overdrive in the fifties. New paintwork, special cleaning – even new loos.

Princess Margaret came, and they built a special toilet for her. The whole town was up in arms. Especially because as soon as she went it was taken away.

The Queen's visit to our town was a major, major event. All the schools sent their pupils to line the streets at designated places, and we all had little Union Jacks to wave. It was very exciting, even though all we saw was a car and an arm in a window, waving. The cavalcade itself was pretty impressive.

We were all given a flag to wave during the Queen's visit, and told to put it on a stick. I forgot to ask my parents in time, and at the last minute my mother gave me a knitting needle. So I had to hold the flag on the knitting-needle stick and wave it as best I could.

"How happy could I be with either !"

CRAWFORD'S SHORTBREAD

. . . and how happy we shall be when this famous Shortbread can be offered in the full quality of its ~~ar~~ excellence.

CHRISTMAS

Christmas held a very special magic in the fifties, and although that sounds like the worst, most schmaltzy cliché ever, it also happens to be true. Christmas in the fifties was the last bastion of naiveté. We believed in Santa Claus coming down the chimney clutching a sack full of presents; we believed in happy families under the mistletoe or gathered around the Christmas tree, in Rudolph and Prancer and Dancer and the rest of the reindeer. We even believed in the little Lord Jesus, asleep in the hay; in the shepherds watching their flocks (or, more cynically, washing their socks) by night; in the three kings following yonder star. The traditions and beliefs of a Christian festival were very much more to the fore, and the crass commercialism we now know was only just beginning to raise its head. Because television wasn't widespread until late in the decade there were no 'Christmas specials' to look forward to; instead, we acted out nativity scenes at school, went carol-singing around the neighbourhood, played charades, made execrable Christmas cards and nativity scenes with cardboard, cotton wool and cellophane paper, and spent the weeks before the day itself in a frenzy of excitement. It really was the biggest event of the year.

Man-about-the-house slippers in tan leather with warm felt linings. 19/11

Put your feet cheerful sli fleecy sol sponge sol In most c

Embroidered bedroom moccasin slippers in a variety of colours— just the thing for chilly mornings. 23/11

The kiddies just love these jolly slippers with Prudence Kitten on the toes. From 9/11

Let Christmas comfort be your gift this year. There's a wonderful range of practical presents at prices you can afford at your local branch of

True-Form

Christmas began every year with carol-singing, about a week before Christmas. That's when we made all our money to buy Christmas presents.

I wish I could relive the excitement of those freezing Christmas mornings, waking in the pre-dawn and tingling with excitement at the day to come. Not just the presents and the food, although of course they were wonderful, but the camaraderie. The socialising – to neighbours' houses for a glass of sherry for grown-ups and cordial or green ginger wine for us; then getting in the car and driving through the snowy, slushy streets to relatives, to exchange presents and drink and eat more. Hearing all the beautiful choirs singing carols, and singing along yourself. And everyone being so jolly and so friendly. It really was the most enjoyable day of the year – better than your birthday, even.

I'd spend the two weeks leading up to Christmas combing the house for presents. I still don't know where Mum used to hide them.

Each year we'd buy a dozen day-old chicks, then on Christmas Eve my father and I would go out the back and slaughter them all for Christmas. That was our Christmas present to our relatives: a chicken. We'd wring their necks then hang them upside down and slit their throats so that they bled to death. Then we'd pluck them.

We had real candles on our Christmas tree, with real flames, clipped onto the ends of branches. Why didn't the house burn down? The decorations were lovely: little glass goldfish, so beautiful.

I always associate cigar smoke with Christmas, because my father had a cigar only on one day of the year, and that was Christmas day. Same with celery: Christmas day was the only day we ever had celery, and the smell of it still reminds me of Christmas.

Christmas was so exciting. So wonderful. I believed in Father Christmas until I was about nine, until someone told me. Like all children then I truly believed that I heard him creeping into the house on Christmas Eve. I didn't get expensive presents, I only ever got one thing plus a stocking. And the stocking always had a mandarin covered in tin foil in the toe; Brazil nuts, which no child actually likes; hazel nuts; some Cadbury's chocolates; little tin stocking fillers; and always a book. And then you'd get the annuals which didn't fit in stockings, such as *Film Fun*, *Radio Fun* and later *Girl's Own* and *Girl's Crystal*.

There were hundreds of us in my family who'd get together at Christmas at my grandparents' house, and we'd all play games such as 'Pass the Ring'. You'd all sit around in a circle, with a piece of string going around everyone, and there was a ring strung on it. You'd all sing, something like 'One Man Went to Mow, Went to Mow a Meadow', and you'd pass this ring along the string from one to another, and the person stood in the middle had to guess who had the ring when you stopped singing. My father said I once accused my grandmother of having it on her finger, and she nearly lost her false teeth laughing.

My parents didn't have much money but there was always plenty of bits and pieces, enough to fill a pillowcase left at the end of the bed. And Dad used to make things for us – little wooden boats, aeroplanes.

I'd get maybe a skirt and jumper on the end of my bed, but nothing was ever wrapped in paper. And there were no bits and pieces either, no stockings. But I didn't feel deprived at all.

"Old Favourites," says Mum

— how well I remember, when I was but little older than Molly is today, the perfect joy of reading my "Strand" and munching my

Mackintosh's

— But Molly has no time for reminiscences. She's all for the present pleasure—especially when it's

Mackintosh's

She thinks their toffees and chocolates are simply wizard, and lets it go at that.

JOHN MACKINTOSH & SONS LTD. HALIFAX

My brother and I had twin beds in this perishing cold bedroom, and our presents were put in a pillowcase on the end of the beds. We always tried desperately to stay awake, but never managed. We'd wake up at half past five and discover this full pillowcase each, and we were allowed to open one thing. Then, shivering with the cold, we took our pillowcases into our parents' bed and we could delve into them and open the rest of the presents.

At eight o'clock on Christmas morning half the street would be out booting around these brand new footballs and things – ruining them, of course, because they weren't meant to be used on tarmac.

Like everybody else we had chicken for Christmas dinner. No one could afford turkey, it just wasn't an option then.

Christmas dinner was like nineteen Sunday lunches rolled into one. There had to be the turkey, the bread and butter sauce, the sprouts, the pudding with the sixpence and the holly on the top. Plus mistletoe, paper chains, fairy lights, Chinese lanterns, Advent calendars. I never made a wish list, because I hoped in an osmotic way that Santa/God would know what I wanted deep down, without being told. Santa just brought you things. But the great thing about Christmas was eating. The big boxes and tins of Cadbury's Roses, Quality Street, that you didn't have much of during the rest of the year. And the nuts, and the oranges.

Boxing Day was our party, and the whole neighbourhood would come over to our place. We'd play games like 'Murder in the Dark' – it was so frightening if you were going to be murdered – and a game where you had to say what you did first thing in the morning. My auntie used to go out the door and, when people answered things like 'I look at the clock', she'd answer, 'Don't you do this?' and pour a jug of water into a bowl, which of course sounded like someone weeing. And everyone cried laughing, because in the fifties this was the height of naughtiness, of daring.

Blackpool Rock and Brighton Pier

HOLIDAYS

Not every family could afford to take holidays: money was tight after the war, rationing was still in place – at least at the beginning of the decade – and not many people had private transport. But many did manage. The idea of the family holiday really took off in the 1950s. And if the holiday wasn't in an exotic resort, and if it consisted of a week in a caravan or boarding house at a dour seaside town or a series of day trips in the rain, it was nevertheless magic for us children. Golden memories of childhood holidays don't need sun, or foreign climes or cuisines; they just need that glorious sense of freedom, of not-school, not-home, of difference – different streets, different smells, different names – to add up to juvenile paradise.

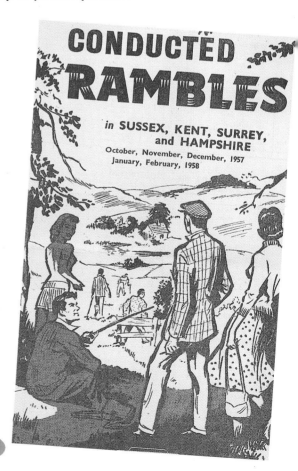

WHERE YOU WILL MEET THE KIND OF PEOPLE YOU'D LIKE TO MEET

On your Butlin holiday you are sure to enjoy yourself among the finest array of entertainments, amusements and amenities obtainable anywhere—and all included in the All-in Tariff. In your sleeping chalet at the edge of the sea and in your dining hall you are surrounded with service. At Butlin's you do no more for yourself than you would expect to do at any first-class hotel. Come to Butlin's this year and enjoy a *real* holiday.

FREE BROCHURE: Send postcard to
BUTLIN'S LTD. (Dept. H.B.), 439 OXFORD STREET, LONDON, W.I

We had summer holidays in cottages in places like Clacton. We took all our stuff there, and the carrier would come and collect all the luggage in advance, in a big tin box. It took seven days for your stuff to get to Munsley or Clacton or wherever. So, for seven days, your best clothes would be in the box, which made them all the more desirable. To this day, I call my favourite clothes my 'luggage in advance' clothes.

We'd have an annual holiday in the caravan site in Llandudno, and Father used to borrow a car for it. People used to do that in those days – lend a car to a friend so they could take their family away on holiday. It seems extraordinary now. It was a very small car, and the four of us would barely fit in. But it was really lovely, I have great memories of these holidays.

We often spent our annual holiday in Devon, which was a 13 or 14 hour drive from where we lived in Yorkshire, with Dad clutching the steering wheel and trying to keep the car going straight, because suspensions in those days weren't quite what they

BOYS' HOLIDA

GILESTON, VALE OF GLAMORGAN, SOUTH WALES

BRITAIN'S first BOYS' HOLIDAY CAMP is now open! The camp aims to give boys of 10 to 15 a happy, healthy seaside holiday under adequate adult supervision The food is plentiful, well cooked and well served. Parents can rest assured that everything possible will be done for their sons' welfare at Gileston. Parents may visit the camp to see their sons by arrangement with the director.

The camp provides holiday adventure and sport for normal healthy boys. The camp staff will do everything in their power to give all boys a very good time. Special couriers escort boys on Saturday trains from London (Paddington), Manchester, Birmingham and Bristol in reserved accommodation.

The terms are £5 per week between July 25 and September 15. By special arrangement members of the B.O.P Club will be charged at a reduced price of £4 per week. Early application should be made as the accommodation for 1951 is strictly limited. Mr. Vernon Jenkins, the Camp Director, will gladly answer any special queries.

B.O.P Competition Story! £100 worth of prizes, including Two Bicycles!

Rex Marks the Spot! is the title of a story especially written at the Boys' Holiday Camp recently by Geoffrey Morgan, B.O.P's Competition Story expert. Read this story carefully and see if YOU can find where the Treasure is hidden. Whether you go to Gileston or not this year you can enter for the Competition and post your entry in accordance with the instructions at the end of the story. The senders of the first TWO CORRECT or NEAREST-CORRECT solutions examined by the Judges on Friday, September 14, 1951, will receive TWO BICYCLES to a value of £15 each, chosen from advertisers in any issue of B.O.P. Senders of the next 15 correct or nearest-correct solutions will each receive ONE WEEK'S FREE HOLIDAY at Gileston in 1952. Enter for this grand competition now! Tell all your friends about it! Hurry!

SEND FOR YOUR BOOKING FORM AT ONCE!

To: THE CAMP DIRECTOR, BOYS' HOLIDAY CAMP, GILESTON,
        VALE OF GLAMORGAN, SOUTH WALES

(Cross out whichever line is not applicable and post at once)

1.   Please send me your illustrated brochure and literature about the BOYS' HOLIDAY CAMP

2.   Please book me provisionally for .... week(s) from .... to ....
      at £5 per week and send me your booking form for completion and return

3.   I am a member of the B.O.P Club, my membership number being .... Please
      book me provisionally for .... week(s) from .... to .... at the
      special privilege price of £4 per week and send me your booking form for completion and return

Name .... Age ....

Address ....
      (in block capitals)

B.O.P. July 1951

are today. We used to stay in what were called 'apartments', where you had your own bedroom and sitting room, and you bought your own food, but the landlady cooked it for you. There was still rationing then, which I think was the main reason for this arrangement, because the landlady couldn't go out and buy food for everyone.

AMP

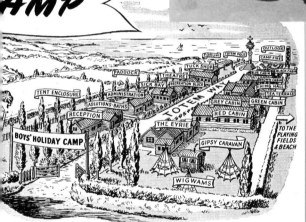

Grand Competition Story!   **£100 worth of Prizes!**

REX MARKS THE SPOT!

by GEOFFREY MORGAN

WHEN Dick Fenton turned the bend in the leafy lane and saw the open white gate and the gaily painted buildings of the Boys' Holiday Camp at Gileston he knew that the picture in the camp brochure had at last come to life.

The camp lay in the beautiful Vale of Glamorgan. The sea was on its doorstep and the wooded slopes of the Welsh countryside rose gently behind it—delightful setting for holiday adventures.

In company with new friends, and escorted by a Camp Courier, who had met them at Birmingham, Dick entered the camp and headed for Reception.

"This is it!" he thought. A fortnight of fun was about to begin.

The camp atmosphere took him back to Redskin encampments. To his right, on a smooth lawn, stood a cluster of wigwams and a gay gipsy caravan. Beyond were "The Eyrie" and the sleeping-cabins—red, grey, green, brown, blue and black, and again beyond these was the camp fire site and a tall lookout tower.

A rose-bordered roadway ran between the cabins and groups of other one-storey buildings on the left. This road was known as Totem Way.

Mum and Dad had a tandem with a sidecar, when I was very small. They went all over the east coast on it with me in the sidecar; there wasn't much traffic. I remember going to Dungeness and riding on the miniature railway they had there – I think it still exists. But apparently when I started standing up and jumping around in the traffic I put a stop to all that.

We couldn't afford to go on a family holiday every year, but regardless of that I used to go on a two-week camp to Bognor Regis with an organisation called the Highgate Camp, which never cost more than £5 all-in. It was organised along old military lines, boys only. It served a purpose, getting some boys away on a break who otherwise wouldn't get away in the school holidays. We had tent inspections, but there was plenty of sport, swimming at the beach. We always had good weather, hot; we'd come back brown. The water always seemed warm.

Southend was a kind of workers' paradise for Londoners, for East Enders, in the fifties. The Kursaal is German for a room where you can have fun, but the Kurzal, as it was called, was considered irredeemably common. Southend Pier, the longest pier in England, was a mile long, with a little railway that ran along its length which used to give me complete nightmares because I was convinced it would one day fall into the sea with me on it. The whole town was full of jellied eels, and cockles and whelks, and candy floss and Southend rock, and fortune tellers and donkey rides, and Punch and Judy shows.

When we got to Filey or Scarborough or wherever, the local children would all be waiting outside the railway station with bogies – trolleys to take luggage off to the boarding houses and digs. Very enterprising.

To be stuck on an English pier must have been truly suicidal for the performers. But to a child, even Punch and Judy people looked so glamorous. The seaside itself was magical. You never seemed to want for entertainment, or food, or deckchairs. The deckchair man would come along with his little ticket roll, and you'd be able to sit in your deckchair for your allotted time.

OUTINGS

Family outings ranged from local walks to day trips into the countryside or to the coast. The spread of the motor car meant the inevitable rise of the 'Sunday driver'.

My parents never did get a car, so we went everywhere by bus. We went to lots of museums. The Commonwealth Institute opened while I was at school, which was a big thing for us. We never bought food while we were out, we always took sandwiches. Occasionally we were allowed to buy a drink, but I always chewed the paper straw to shreds, which drove my father insane, so we didn't get them very often.

We went on lots of outings to Blackpool, Morecambe and Southport, by train because we didn't have a car. Lots of fun to be had: donkey rides, sandcastles, ice creams, candy floss, fun fairs. It was always wonderful, amazing. We loved it.

Not all northern towns had holidays at the same time, because it wouldn't do to have all of Bury, Bolton, Wigan and Preston to go to Blackpool together. So Wigan had holidays at the same time as places like Glasgow. It was a very volatile arrangement – there were horrendous fights, drunken evenings. I've never had so much tremendous fun as when I sat on the boarding house steps in Blackpool singing with the drunks from Glasgow.

Focus on
BRIGHTON
AND HOVE

We always had a car: a Ford Prefect, then a Vauxhall Viva, a Vauxhall Wyverne. They were biggish, bulbous cars with leather seats, lots of chrome and wooden dashboards. We used to go out to Breedon on the Hill, to watch the cricket. There was a canteen and paddling pool and a picnic area. I have lots of

SUNDAY EXCURSIONS

FROM

PADDINGTON

AND

EALING BROADWAY

DURING

DECEMBER, 1957

Paddington Station, W.2.
October, 1957.

K. W. C. GRAND,
General Manager.

WESTERN — BRITISH RAILWAYS — REGION

JENNI MURRAY (B.1950)

When I began researching my history of women since 1945 I came across a *Woman's Weekly* of 1954 (I was four then) which came with the paper every Tuesday. In it was a pattern –THE pattern – for the knitted swimsuit my mother made for me. Suddenly I was back on the beach at Scarborough. Grandpa in his shirt, tie, socks and sandals. Grandma with crimped white hair, flowery frock, and a little too much foundation. Mum in a crisp shirtwaister, daddy handsome and slender in immaculate white flannels – all in stripy deckchairs in a chill wind. And little me leaping over the icy waves of the North Sea as the woollen cossie became weightier and weightier and finally slipped down to expose – oh horror – my chest!

photos of The Picnic – the cloth spread on the grass, and my mother in her sundress with a gathered top and a big flowery skirt, posing with the basket and all its special picnic cutlery, and Thermos flasks, and chicken legs, and egg and cress sandwiches with the crusts all cut off. We children were left to amuse ourselves, more or less.

Outings in those days weren't as frequent or as expected as now. Parents didn't feel obliged to keep children moving in the same way; parents then didn't see it as their life's obligation to keep us entertained. The idea was to keep us socialised and obedient.

We'd go to the Epsom Derby every year. That was a big day out. There was an amazing character there called Prince Monolulu, a bookmaker. We were allowed to have a bet on the Derby, and one year I won. The horse was called Hard Ridden, I think, and he was about 20-1. I had threepence each way on him – it was a Big Bet. When you only got a penny a week pocket money, threepence each way was a Big Bet. So I won a lot of money, and I've been a gambler ever since.

GETTING AROUND
We were far more reliant on public transport in the fifties. Sometimes it was wonderful, but at other times it left an awful lot to be desired.

We'd go to school on the trolley bus. Trolley buses were excellent because you could listen to the post, and the sound would tell you how close it was. But every other trip the antennae, or whatever they were called – those big feelers that stuck out the top of the bus and attached to the lines – would come off at a particular corner, and it would take ages for the conductor to get them back on again. And sometimes they would crackle just like lightning.

The bus conductor would have a long row of different tickets in little containers slung around his neck, and he'd pull one out and punch it before handing it to you. If you went upstairs on the bus you'd be practically asphyxiated, because everybody smoked up there. But it was worth it because it was much more exciting upstairs.

The Oxford accent is on *Quality*

In its modern styling, the excellence of its performance, comfort, roomy seating, generous luggage space and fine finish the "Quality First" Morris Oxford has everything that makes for lasting pride in ownership.

The "Quality First" **MORRIS** *Oxford*

Morris Motors Limited, Cowley, Oxford. Export: Nuffield Exports Ltd., Oxford & 41 Piccadilly, W.1

I spent my first train ride, apparently, banging on the doors and screaming to be let out. I think mainly because the train was so disgustingly smelly with cigarette smoke and unwashed bodies. Public transport then was really rather gross. You'd finish up a train ride with your mouth and nostrils choked up with coal dust and smoke, and buses, especially the double-deckers, were indescribable.

'Hello, children, everywhere'
The media and us

I loved the stories in *Girl's Crystal*, 'The Three Marys', and the stories of being in girls' schools. The endless stories of the orphan who was brought up by the wicked and cruel

BOOKS AND LITERATURE
In pre-television days books and comics were all the more important. Once we were over the book-torturing toddler stage books became prized objects, the only medium other than radio and infrequent films able to transport us away from the mundane into wonderful imaginary worlds. Enid Blyton seems to have been our favourite author by a huge margin.

and dismissive family, who turned out to be the rich person's daughter or the princess; we all wanted to be that. The joy of getting the annual, and sneaking back upstairs to read it.

Annuals were really important. We used to get the *Girl* annuals, and the *Swift* annuals. But we were definitely told that Enid Blyton wasn't quite what was approved of. So I'd always try to borrow her books from friends and read them illicitly.

I read all the G. A. Henty books, which were called 'Books for Boys', despite the fact that I was a girl. Books like *With Clive in India*. There was a boys' shelf in the library, and I got right into those books.

One of Noel Streatfield's books featured a heroine who could fly a plane and became a pilot, and that was such a role model for me. Mostly, books featured girls who lived in enormous houses or went away to boarding school, whose fathers were away in India or wherever, and I couldn't relate to them at all. I never read a book about a school where people lived in ordinary families, in ordinary homes.

All girls in books were uniformly silly and soppy, apart from George in the *Famous Five* books and William Brown's friend Joan in the *Just William* books.

Whenever a new Noddy book came out, my father would buy it and bring it home for me. I particularly remember number seven, *Noddy by the Seaside*, because I'd been waiting for it for so long. It was pale blue.

I was desperate to have the same sorts of adventures the children in Enid Blyton books had. I loved the *Famous Five* books, but best of all were the *Adventure* series: *The*

Mountain of Adventure, The Sea of Adventure, The Island of Adventure, and so on. I still think they were every bit as exciting as *Raiders of the Lost Ark.* Anyway, I wanted to have those adventures, so for years I diligently made sure that my pockets were full of such useful items as string, compass, pocket knife, notebook, pencil, etc, in readiness for being kidnapped, or coming across escaped criminals, or a bank robbery in progress, or whatever. Needless to say . . .

My play world was based entirely upon the adventure model. I didn't read any of the classics such as *The Wind in the Willows* or *Swallows and Amazons.* I read stuff on my parents' bookshelves – stuff they told me not to read, such as *The Tribe That Lost its Head* by Nicholas Montserrat, and *The Seven Pillars of Wisdom* by T.E. Lawrence, and *The Singer Not the Song* by Audrey Erskine Winthrop, set in South America, which I read three times, I was completely enthralled by it.

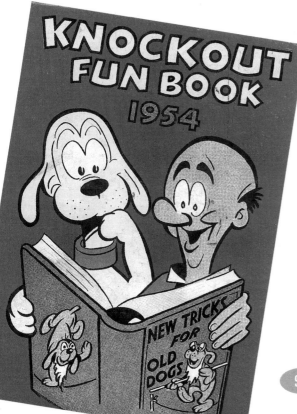

I read all the time as a child. Most books came from the library – my brother and I would go to confession at St Coleman's church on Saturday morning with my dad – then on to the library – new souls, new books each week! My own most precious books were *Little Women, What Katy Did, What Katy Did at School* and *What Katy Did Next.* Also, of course, I had *Little Men, Good Wives* and *Jo's Boys.*

My cousin used to send me her old annuals – I didn't care a bit that they were last year's books. The excitement of opening that parcel and seeing the covers!

COMICS
Comics provided enormous fun and enjoyment, but were often frowned upon and even banned by well-meaning parents who had no idea what the term would encompass in subsequent years.

Tuesday night was comic night. My sister and I would spend the early evening at our Nana's, and the excitement began when the comics were delivered at about 5 o'clock. The glorious sound of those magazines hitting the floor as they came through the letterbox! We'd get *Chick's Own,* then *Dandy* and *Beano,* later *Girl* and *Bunty.* They were all such a joy.

I used to read *Sunny Stories* when I was very small, then I had *Girl.* My brother had *Eagle.* You could hear them being delivered, because there was no other background sound.

We were given something called *The Children's Newspaper* which was extremely tedious. Terrible. We wanted *Dandy* and *Beano,* but we weren't allowed to have them.

I had to fight to get the *Beezer*. Before that, I was allowed to get *Girl*. I looked down on *Bunty* because my parents did.

I got loads of comics, because my mother worked in the local newsagent's. They were all last week's, but who cared. There was *Lion*, and *Eagle*, and *Rover* and *Adventure*, and then *Rover Adventure* because they'd merged. I read them all avidly, cover to cover, except for the obligatory 'educational' feature in the middle, about butterflies or whatever. The Bash Street Kids were my favourite. Lord Snooty. Keyhole Kate.

POSY SIMMONDS
(B. 1945)

My Fifties

From our home in rural Cookham we would go to London for our holidays. London was so filthy then, when you got back you had black bogeys. And smuts. And you always gave your newspaper to the engine driver of the train. It seemed to be expected.

The most exciting thing was getting to know American children at the air base nearby. Americans seemed so glamorous: they gave us Hershey bars and Coca-Cola and American comics with Superman and Sad Sack and Caspar the Ghost. At home we had *Dandy, Beano, Robin, Swift, Eagle* and *Girl*. I preferred *Wendy* to *Jinx*; Wendy's hair was black with a blue sheen on it. I thought *Belle of the Ballet* a bit wet. I called her Belly.

Most of all I adored Willans and Searle's *Molesworth* books, *How to be Topp*, etc. We all went around saying 'Chiz chiz' and calling people Fotherington-Thomas (the utterly weedy wet).

The best thing about the end of the 1950s was getting to join Yardley's Teenage Club, which sent you samples of bright pink lipstick. Pink Magic was my colour: I slapped it on.

What we listened to

Sounds were all important in the days before television. The radio was a wonderful source of stories and music

RADIO

'It's quarter to two, Mummy! Quarter to two!' This was the catchcry of our early childhood, as we made sure that our mother had the radio tuned to our programme and the armchairs and cushions plumped ready for that magical time, 'Listen With Mother'. For half an hour, we'd be lost in the stories, songs and poems featuring such creatures as Greedy Harry Biggs, Dan Pig ('that did make Dan Pig laugh! Ho ho ho!') and the farmer whose horse fell down into a ditch. Later, Saturday mornings were devoted to Uncle Mac and his lovely programme 'Children's Favourites'.

'Listen With Mother' is almost chillingly familiar. It brings back such intense memories. There was always a story, and I remember one in particular. It was about a little girl who has to go shopping for her mother, and she makes up a song about the shopping list. It went like this:

'Nutmeg, ginger, cinnamon and mace
Nutmeg, ginger, cinnamon and mace.'

To this day, I recite shopping lists in my mind in exactly the same way. 'Stamps, string, bank, peas.' Make them into groups of four or five, and sing them to myself.

I loved 'Children's Hour'. I used to listen to David Davis, he read all the long children's stories, the serials. The sound of his voice brings back to me all that stuff about dark Sundays – he must have read the stories on Sundays. An amazing voice.

I remember the joy of huddling in front of the fire at night, in a darkened room, and listening to someone to telling you stories such as 'Larry the Lamb' and 'Toytown' out of the huge old Bakelite radio with gold mesh speakers.

DEBORAH MOGGACH (B. 1948)

My Fifties

Pre-central heating, I remember the repeated chorus of 'Close the DOOR!' Chilblains, arctic lavatories and Bronco. The magic of side-indicators popping out of cars. The thrilling luxury of roast chicken and frozen peas! Nobody drinking, except a sherry before Sunday lunch. People whistling and singing in the street. Pervasive dowdiness, and lack of choice, but children only realise that later, and who cared?

I remember the science fiction programme on Sunday nights, 'Journey Into Space '– it scared the hell out of me. I used to stuff things in my ears but I still couldn't miss it, it was the highlight of the week. Absolutely tremendous!

I remember 'The Billy Cotton Band Show' being on the radio, just as Sunday lunch was about to be eaten. 'Wakey wa-a-a-key!' And 'The Goon Show' was something I never missed.

Daddy used to make our radios for us, he made crystal sets with headphones. And 'Saturday Night Theatre' would come on at 8.45 or 9.45 and go on until 10.45, which was really late, and in bed I would listen to a whole lot of really frightening stuff through these headphones, like 'Dr Jekyll and Mr Hyde'. You had to listen through the headphones, because there was no on and off button, the radio was on all the time, only you couldn't hear it unless you had the headphones on. I used to think my father was magic, because of course as soon as you heard him coming you'd take the headphones off and feign sleep. He always knew, miraculously, if I'd had the headphones on. And I only realised ages afterwards that he'd felt the headphones, and if they were warm he'd know I'd just used them.

I loved the Glums on 'Take it From Here':
'Take it from here
Don't go away when you can take it from here.'
Dick Bentley and June Whitfield, as Ron and Eth.

At three o'clock on Sundays there was 'Movie Go-Round', with the theme music from *Carousel*, and it was very exciting because you could hear clips from films. The radio was a really big thing. We were radio-dependent. We marked the stages of our days by the radio, just as we do by our watches today. It was always on, never off.

MAGIC MOMENTS
Words by HAL DAVID   Music by BURT F. BACHARACH

RECORDED ON R.C.A. VICTOR RECORDS BY
PERRY COMO

I loved 'Top of the Form'. It was always recorded in a school hall and it was always boys versus girls, and at the end of every round the audience all had to shout 'Come on the boys!' or 'Come on the girls!' And we'd do this in our home; my brother and I would shout 'Come on the boys!' and Mam would shout 'Come on the girls!'

MUSIC AND RECORDS
As the decade progressed, we began hearing and buying records – a magical new sound called rock 'n' roll.

There was something very innocent and wholesome about the songs that were popular in the fifties. 'Sippin' Soda' and 'Singin' the Blues' by Guy Mitchell, 'A Four-legged Friend' by Roy Rogers, 'Secret Love' by Doris Day. Then there was 'The Tennessee Wig Walk', and you could do all the movements to it as you sang along.

I remember the 'Ovaltineys'. Saturday night, I think. And 'Round the Horne'. But we never listened to 'The Goon Show'. The radio was rented, from Radio Rentals. Just like the television was, when we eventually got one in 1958.

We had a family ritual of always listening to 'The Archers'. We used to sit every night and listen. We never listened to 'Mrs Dale's Diary'.

'Educating Archie' with Peter Brough was terrible. Can you imagine, a ventriloquist on radio. Such an absurd concept!

WHATEVER WILL B QUE SERA, SERA
by JAY LIVINGSTON & RAY EVANS

PARAMOUNT PRESENTS
JAMES STEWART
DORIS DAY
IN ALFRED HITCHCOCK'S
"THE MAN WHO KNEW TOO MUCH"
VISTAVISION
COLOUR BY TECHNICOLOR
DIRECTED BY ALFRED HITCHCOCK
SCREENPLAY BY JOHN MICHAEL HAYES
BASED ON A STORY BY CHARLES BENNETT AND D.B. WYNDHAM LEWIS

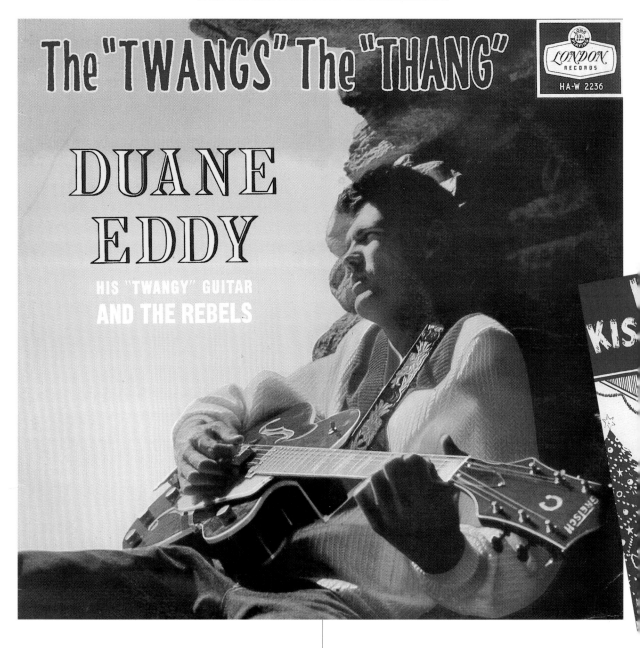

The "TWANGS" The "THANG"

DUANE EDDY

HIS "TWANGY" GUITAR
AND THE REBELS

LONDON RECORDS
HA-W 2236

KIS

Records were expensive, and they broke, and they scratched. They cost 7/6, then very quickly 10 bob, when people were only earning about ten quid a week, and when you stood on one or sat on one that was the end of it.

I had an old wind-up record player from my grandmother, with all the old 78s. Things like 'The Laughing Policeman', old music hall stuff. I played them non-stop. My mother hated them and said she'd throw them all out if I didn't stop playing them. I had a bow and arrow, so I took all the records and put them up on the fence and smashed them with my bow and arrow. Everyone was pleased, but that record collection would now be worth hundreds of thousands.

The records that got into me were the records my parents bought. We had Frank Sinatra, *Songs for Swinging Lovers*, with 'Wee Small Hours of the Morning' on it; we had the musicals – *Oklahoma*, *South Pacific*, *Kismet*, *Dancing Years*, *Kiss Me Kate*. I'm a singer now,

and that's where I get my repertoire from. Frank Sinatra, Lena Horne, Ella Fitzgerald. The one I most remember is Lena Horne's 'Honeysuckle Rose'; on the other side she sang 'Newfangled Tango'. 'Honeysuckle Rose' had sex in every line, a basic swing standard – I just loved it. Ella Fitzgerald's 'Midnight Sun' is just beautiful, you hardly ever hear it nowadays. And there were people like David Whitfield, who until quite recently was performing in pubs in north Wales, and Frankie Lane – an amazing voice. I have an album of his called *That's My Desire*. Of course, I rejected all this music later, in the sixties, but I came back to it.

I was very keen on skiffle when it came out. Lonnie Donegan. Until then I hadn't really been interested in the music played on the radio. We formed a group and played at our school, with a washboard and everything. I got Acker Bilk's autograph, later on.

The first record I ever bought was *Heartbreak Hotel* by Elvis, which came out in 1956. It really was an extraordinary new sound, so thrilling. My parents were appalled.

What we watched

Until television sets became more commonplace in the latter half of the decade, the cinema reigned supreme as the place where we could see new and fantastic worlds.

Nothing will ever compete with the sheer glamour of the films and film stars of the 1950s. The very titles of the films – *Carve Her Name With Pride, The Guns of Navarone, High Noon, Seagulls Over Sorrento, Bad Day at Black Rock* – and the names of the stars – Gary Cooper, Ava Gardner, John Wayne, Jane Russell – still send a shiver down my spine.

Our parents took us to see *Fantasia* when it first came out. We were too young to appreciate it – I remember enjoying the animal sequences, especially the dancing hippos, but the satyrs were beyond me and most of the music bored me. My sister and I squirmed so much we nearly forced our parents to take us home – but I'm glad we didn't succeed, because I still remember the power of *Night on a Bare Mountain* at the end.

Saturday morning cinema was like another world, which I wasn't usually allowed into. There were hundreds of people there, all shouting and bawling. It was just like a general riot, really. A little man used to come on in front of the curtains and try to do things like hula-hoop competitions. He had no chance. Then we all had to sing the Saturday morning cinema song; then we'd all make terrible animal noises and throw things.

icture Show & FILM PICTORIAL

July 24th, 1954 Vol. 63 No. 1636 Every Tuesday 3D

PAPER FOR PEOPLE WHO GO TO THE PICTURES

ST. JOHN
MONTALBAN

Going to the pictures was just going out, it wasn't about going to see a particular film. It didn't really matter what was showing. It felt grown-up. Mum, Dad and I used to go every Friday evening and sit in the same three seats in the middle of the cinema.

I went to see *Lassie* but I cried so much I had to come out, it was so upsetting.

I loved the epic films of the fifties, and the war films. *The Dam Busters* was my favourite, then later *Ben Hur*.

I thought the Norman Wisdom films were so funny. I think I'd probably squirm with embarrassment if I saw them now, but at the time they were hilarious.

There was a bit of a competition between local cinemas. You could join the Odeon Club, or the Gaumont Club, show your allegiance and be rewarded. We even had a song, I sang it with Rod Stewart once at a Christmas soccer do. It went
'We come along on a Saturday morning
Greeting everybody with a smile
We come along on a Saturday morning
Knowing that it's all worthwhile
As members of the Odeon Club
We all intend to be
Good citizens when we grow up
And champions of the free.'
We had to sing that before the show started, and the National Anthem.

My Fifties

SIR DAVID HARE
(B. 1947)

Dirk Bogarde as Simon Sparrow in *Doctor in the House*: not just the last word in urbanity, but also the last moment in history when people were able to believe that getting the girl (in this case Muriel Pavlow) was the end of the adventure, rather than the beginning.

The first horror films we saw were so terrifying. *The Hound of the Baskervilles*, and *The Pit and the Pendulum*. Would they be as scary today? Probably not, but we weren't used to seeing such things then. It was a new thing for children.

STAGE SHOWS

Theatre outings were a rare treat for most of us in the fifties. Pantomimes were traditional at Christmas, and most towns had a visit from a circus during the year. Then came pop concerts.

We used to go to Richmond Theatre, and the theatre in town. We also used to go and see Billy Smart's Circus at Olympia, and that was really exciting. It was tenpence, and we took the 267 from the top of the road all the way to Olympia. The flea circus was the best.

COSY NOOK - NEWQUA

Proprietors NEWQUAY URBAN DISTRICT COUNCIL
Lessees HEDLEY CLAXTON PRODUCTIONS LTD.
Manager RONNIE MASTERS
Telephone NEWQUAY 3365

Hedley Claxton
presents

GAYTIME

A SPARKLING SUMMER SHOW

ROLLETT

SOUVENIR PROGRAMME

SIXPENCE

CHU CHIN CHOW ON ICE

The world-famous musical tale of the East, told in the modern manner

EMPIRE POOL WEMBLEY

The amateur dramatic society in the village put on lots of plays, nearly all farces – Brian Rix-type stuff. *The Cuckoo's Nest* or something like that was one. That's where my Uncle Horace met my Auntie Margaret. I imagine that most of them were ghastly, but I was no judge as a child.

On our annual holidays in Scarborough we'd go to the rep shows and watch people like Ken Dodd. Always a bit of a laugh.

The annual Christmas pantomime was a real treat. I remember one where we children had to call out 'I'm as daft as a brush!' all the time. Great fun!

By the end of the fifties my friends and I were going to see pop singers on stage: Wee Willie Harris, Eddie Cochrane, and Jerry Lee Lewis.

TELEVISION
The coming of the television set into nearly every household in the land was undoubtedly the biggest and most influential social phenomenon of the decade. It changed our lives.

My father actually made our first television set, in the early fifties. I remember playing out in the garden with my sister and being called in because the television was working. So we rushed inside, really excited, and drew the curtains, and Daddy turned the television on, and instead of a picture there was one of those green dots you used to get in the middle of the set. That was it. We were bitterly disappointed.

"You and your MacDonald Hobley! Are we eloping or are we not?"

We loved all the children's programmes of the fifties. We started with 'Watch With Mother': Rag, Tag and Bobtail, Muffin the Mule, The Flowerpot Men, Andy Pandy, The Woodentops – who could ever forget the two children dancing and prancing around singing 'Peas for dinner! Peas for dinner!' rapturously – then graduated to 'Crackerjack' and the Huw Wheldon science programmes. Great stuff. You got a cabbage to carry on 'Crackerjack' if you got a question wrong, and people ended up in such straits!

The whole neighbourhood used to congregate in the front room of the one household in the street to have television in the mid-fifties. We'd watch 'Children's Hour'. One girl's mother always came with her and drove the rest of us batty, because being used to radio she'd describe everything that was happening on screen, loudly, all the time, as if we couldn't see it for ourselves.

The first programme I remember watching and enjoying is 'Lost in Space'. But it frightened me. It was a serial. I had to have the light left on when I went to bed after that was on.

Sylvia Peters was so glamorous and wonderful, wearing her evening dresses. 'Good evening, viewers.' She had a perfect heart-shaped face. Gilbert Harding, on the other hand, was so gruff.

On Sundays there was a programme called 'All Your Own' with Huw Wheldon, and children who had made cathedrals out of matchsticks would come on and show us how clever they were. The child we despised most was a girl with bunches in her hair who did Irish dancing with her hands by her side. We found that so annoying. Huw Wheldon would thank everyone at the end and say that he hoped we'd watch next week the programme that was 'well and truly, all your own'.

I hated 'The Brains Trust'. My parents and uncle all used to sit and watch this, so I did too, and I just didn't understand it. I suppose it was like current affairs programmes now.

Eamon Andrews seemed to be in every television programme broadcast during the 1950s: 'What's My Line?', 'Crackerjack', and about a hundred more. He was a more familiar figure than most of my far-flung relatives – a part of the family, despite the Irish accent.

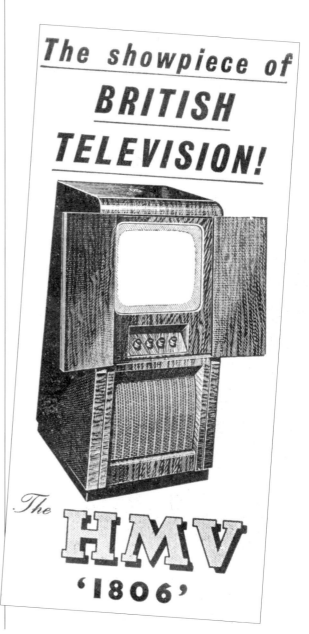

The showpiece of BRITISH TELEVISION!

The HMV '1806'

Postscript: the end of the age of innocence

GROWING UP

By the end of the fifties our teenage years were on us, or loomed large, and things were never to be the same again. The unprecedented freedom and largesse we had enjoyed as children led to us being the first generation to really have a 'teenage'. And we certainly made the most of it.

My friends were all a year older than me so when I was eleven they all had their Louis heels and make-up, and I couldn't have those things. Then I began to paint my nails because my sister did, and shave my legs because my sister did, and before I knew it I was a teenager.

I always played with the neighbourhood boys, not girls, because I found them more interesting. I wanted to kick footballs and climb trees. Then one day when I was about eleven I painted my nails, because I'd seen my sister do it, and the boys turned on me nastily. They ganged up on me in the shed, held me down and cut all my nails off with a pair of clippers. Tomboys weren't allowed to become girls. Of course, later they did allow me to become a girl, once they realized what it was all about.

My mother let me into the Big Secret by giving me a little book one day when I was eleven. It was in a brown envelope and it came, I noticed, from *Woman*, the magazine she read.

Intriguing. She told me to read it and then come and ask her anything I did not understand. The trouble was that I did not understand a word of it. What I read was all about ashes: the body of a woman cleaning out its own ashes once a month, and not to be frightened by it as it was a purifying process. I failed to see the word 'blood' because I'd already got the image of ashes – as we cleaned the grate out every day – lodged firmly in my mind.

In our day we were more embarrassed by periods than anything else. It would have been much easier if we could have discussed it with each other. In the days of the sanitary towel, which you carried to school at the bottom of your satchel in a crumpled brown paper bag so it got squashed beneath homework and littered with pencil shavings and ink stains, you were instructed to burn them in the incinerator rather than flush them away. There can be no more irrational and silly fear than waiting in the toilet cubicle till the last voice had gone so I could dash out and tip the dreaded thing into the incinerator when no one was looking.

My friend and I each had a gang, we were top girls at our primary school. Then I went to her birthday party and we had to play 'Postman's Knock', which involved going outside the room and kissing a boy in the hall. I found this quite frightening. So was 'Forfeits' – I always worried that this would involve removing some item of clothing. And I was right, it usually did.

Sex was never, ever mentioned when I was a child. Never. It was evil, dirty, never to be discussed. So I spent my time playing outdoors, never thinking about girls until I was about sixteen. I was just a happy, sports-mad kid.

In the late fifties, when I was 11 or 12 and my sister a year older, we started going to parties with the local kids and playing games like 'Spin the Bottle' and 'Postman's Knock', and ending up with the lights switched off and everyone coupled off – just for 'necking', nothing more. One time we both got home a little flushed and a little worried about what our parents would say, but all those trivial worries were swept away in a tidal wave of horror when we learnt on arrival that our dog had been run over that night. It put all that stuff into perspective for us.

I remember trying to scream at the pop stars – well, we did scream. My school beret went up in the air during one of the Elvis films, and was never seen again. And dancing in the aisles. *Loving You* was my favourite film for ages. And *Jailhouse Rock*.

FIRST LOVE
As ever, first love was agony and ecstasy.

The first date I ever had was in 1959. I was 12, and we went to see *The World, the Flesh and the Devil,* an X-rated film. After saying hello we didn't exchange another word all evening, not even when I fell down the stairs twice coming out of the cinema because of the ridiculous high heels I was wearing. We never went out together again.

A boy called Martin used to walk me home from the swimming baths every Thursday night, and he'd stop in the park and say, 'Shall we?', meaning kiss.

I received my first Valentine card in 1959, when I was 11. It had inside a handwritten verse:
'I loved you then,
I love you still,
But darling, no more –
I never will.'
Well, he never did, because to this day I don't know who sent it, or why, or what exactly it meant.

I met my first love at the church youth club. That was the best thing about going to Sunday School: eventually, it turned into the youth club, and you met boys and started snogging.

I remember the girls' changing rooms with girls smearing on lipstick and puffing up their hair, backcombing it then spraying it with awful-smelling hairspray.

I was gripped by people kissing on television. It was a fascination linked with horror. I wondered for many years whether, to be kissed, the woman had to put her arms up loosely around the man's neck and accept his head coming down on hers while she leaned backwards.

My first boyfriend was a terrible poseur *who dressed like a Teddy boy but was really very wimpish and shy. He wore drainpipe trousers and fluorescent socks and a jacket with a velvet collar. I tried to dress like his moll but my heart wasn't really in it – and I was too young, anyway.*

BAD HABITS
Our major bad habit was smoking.

My friend Ann began smoking when she was about ten. We'd scour the gutters of our home town, looking for dumpers. Sometimes you'd get half an inch, or even an inch, of unsmoked cigarette. I didn't smoke myself, but I aided and abetted her.

I began smoking when I was about nine or ten. In those days you could buy single cigarettes, Woodbines or Senior Service, from the corner shops, no questions asked. I used to put bits of cotton wool in my boxes of matches so they didn't rattle when I was at home. My clothes and hair must have smelt of tobacco, but my parents didn't seem to notice. Of course, they both smoked too.

At some stage, we turned into scheming little harridans, wearing high heels and bright red lipstick and striking poses wherever we could. But it was all still very innocent – we had no real idea of the consequences of what we were doing. That came later.

On the way back from the local dance hall – we were allowed to go there in the late fifties, even though we were barely into our teens – the boys would end up scrawling filthy drawings on the garage doors in the laneways. An early form of graffiti.

All of a sudden there were lots of teenage dances. They all had a last waltz, and it was terribly important to dance the last waltz with the right boy.

There was a dance hall my sister and I started going to at a really early age, pre-teen, towards the end of the fifties. The boys there almost jitterbugged rather than jived, in trousers that flapped around their legs. It was an incredibly sexy place, looking back.

I remember the first time I got dressed especially to impress a boy at the church youth club. This involved wearing an awful dress that had no sleeves and layers of purple frills, and I had to buy a purple velvet headband to match. Because I had to get him. Lots of backcombing the hair, and lots of lacquer. It didn't work. He didn't fancy me at all.

Brave new world

There was such a feeling of 'Brave New World' about the fifties. Everything seemed wonderfully clean and fresh and bright and new. We were clean and healthy, clothes were clean, mothers wore bright red lipstick.

We were at the beginning of the push to get as many boys and girls as possible into the redbrick universities. Boys and girls from working-class homes, with parents who had no academic aspirations, were now seeing themselves as university fodder. Girls whose mothers had never imagined them as anything more than secretaries were being caught up in the tide of enthusiasm.

We also wanted to have fun. We did not want to be like the prefects of two or three years ahead – they seemed drab and boring, girls who had sacrificed their lives to getting on at school. We had this notion that it was possible for us to be clever, witty and bad, and still do well at school.

We were definitely brought up in the best of times. Even twenty years earlier, I'd have ended up as a drudge; fifty years earlier, I'd have been a tweenie. The post-war years opened countless doors for us children of Britain, and I like to think that we're still aware of that, still appreciate what a charmed life we've led.

the sixties contents

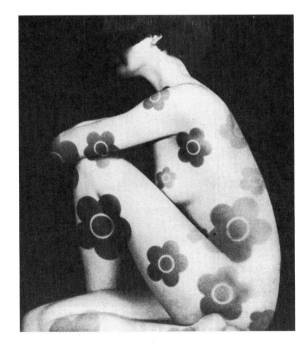

Everything had felt so Victorian in the fifties. It really was as though everything burst into colour when the sixties and the Beatles and their music came along.

1960 was a changeover year in my life, from the dagginess of being a child in the fifties in that monochrome world to a world full of excitement. The satire boom happened around then. It was a period of becoming genuinely politically aware. You started the sixties drinking Vimto and by the end you were drinking crème de menthe.

Generally, there was a feeling of 'we can have a good time for as long as we want'. It was an endless party. Getting a job and other such issues were on the sideline.

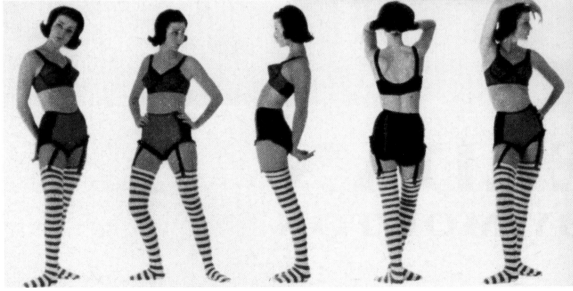

23rd APRIL 1966
ONE SHILLING

for the young and fancy free

petticoat

Beauty stays clinging ... Sweater Dresses go swinging ... and Undies get a new break

the spirit

You were absolutely allowed to have fun and experiment. Generally speaking, everyone was having a good time. There were lots of parties, with masses to drink and decorations all over the place. There was no sense it was going to end; none at all.

Experimentation. The feeling that you could live on the edge, that it was wide open, that you were actually living in a very interesting time. Maybe you were just lucky that all these things were happening. There was lots of style, lots of things were happening, and it was all worth involving yourself in.

As a period in history, it did seem like a huge liberation. It seemed to belong to the young, and I was one of them. Even then, I was aware of being in the right place at the right time, and there was a certain pleasure in knowing that.

It was the feeling that you could wake up in the morning and think of an amazing idea, and you could do it. Nothing was daunting, everything was possible. People

AUTOMATIC TELESCOPE

weren't hindered by their accents any more, whether they were northern or Cockney or Antipodean or whatever – in fact an accent was an advantage, for the first time ever. There was a recognition that it was what you did, not who you were or what your voice said about you, that was important.

Regional awareness came in with the Liverpool thing, the Newcastle thing. Suddenly, it wasn't a source of shame that you came from somewhere north of Watford. Suddenly, there was the world, and you could go and join it.

PHILIP NORMAN

Philip Norman, biographer of the Beatles, Buddy Holly and Elton John, was a provincial journalist in Darlington until 1966 when he won, with a profile of his grandma, a feature-writing job on The Sunday Times Magazine. In his Beatles biography he says: 'For those who grew up in the 1960s, 1967 is a year to be remembered above any other, the moment when their own youth reached a dazzling and careless apogee, the year of love, peace and flower-power.'

"As a rule, only war, or some fearful tragedy, can penetrate the preoccupations of millions in the same moment to produce a single, concerted emotion. And yet, in June 1967, such an emotion arose, not from death or trepidation, but from the playing of a gramophone record. There are, to this day, thousands of Britons and Americans who can describe exactly where they were and what they were doing at the moment they first listened to Sergeant Pepper's Lonely Hearts Club Band. That music, as powerfully as Kennedy's assassination or the first moon landing, summons up an exact time and place, an emotion undimmed by time or ageing."

...DAYS I'LL REMEMBER...

It was a bit of a blur. It just rolled on.

We grew up assuming we could have our freedom and adventures, and come out unscathed, didn't we?

What we didn't know was that it was The Sixties. We just thought, 'well, here it is and here I am'. There'd been the Depression, then the War, then the age of austerity, and now, we felt, 'it's going to be good for ever and ever'. We didn't think, 'oh, I expect it'll go back to being dreary'. We thought, 'goody, we've solved things'.

the spirit

I was very aware that it was a significant era. I thought we were the bee's knees. I thought we were the first people ever to be like that, we'd broken all conventions, we were going to change the world, we were untouchable. I thought everyone who came before us had missed out. We were dead lucky. Nothing would ever be the same again, and my generation had done it. I was living in the best times there had ever been, and my generation was the best that had ever lived. We thought differently, we were different – no question.

I can't think of a better time to have been young. Everything was still so naughty: you didn't easily grow your hair, you didn't easily smoke pot, you didn't easily leave home; you didn't easily tell your parents that you were going to live with a girl or that you were gay. So many things that you did, like going to a pop concert or hitchhiking or wearing funny clothes, were considered on the edge; you were being deliberately rebellious.

It was a good time, wasn't it?

It was fab!

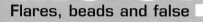
The look

Our appearance—the clothes we wore, how we arranged our hair, what we slapped or grew on our faces—was what the sixties were all about. This was what distinguished us from 'them', the pitiable people who didn't belong to our generation. As soon as we were let loose from smocked party dresses and navy serge short trousers we gleefully invented our own special look. It started in the late fifties with the full skirts and drainpipe trousers of rock 'n' roll, gathered momentum in the mid sixties when psychedelia meant we went out looking like optical illusions, and came to fruition in the late sixties in a cloud of floating chiffon, beads, jangling bells, bell-bottoms, sequins and embroidered kaftans. We left a trail of flowers in our wake.

From the fifties...

The fifties was an era of poverty, and a hangover from the war; dullness, essentially, despite the beginning of rock 'n' roll. Fashions seemed prissy, hairstyles were horrible. With the sixties, in came long straight hair, black polo-necked sweaters, skinny ribs – a more interesting time.

I couldn't wait to get into a roll-on. I'd watch the older girls at school enviously as they changed for PE. Then the minute I was old enough, tights came in and roll-ons rolled away forever, and I never did get to squeeze myself into a corset. I could do with one now, though.

When tights first came onto the market, I never knew whether you should wear them under or over your knickers. It was never very plain, was it? And there were two schools of thought about it. I was seriously worried at the time.

When I was fourteen, in 1961, my school organized a Christmas dance. My aunt was staying with us at the time, from the deep north, and she and my mother said they'd go shopping for a dress for me. I got home from school on the day of the dance, all agog, and found that they'd bought me a frilly little girl's dress. I knew how much it hurt them, but I just couldn't face going to the dance in that revolting dress. So I ended up going in my usual weekend wear, a checked skirt and striped top, feeling ordinary but at least not mortified. They were genuinely trying to do the right thing – they just had no idea that times had changed.

I spent most of the weekends of my mid-teens slobbing around my long-suffering parents' house in a smelly, stained, pale blue, quilted, nylon housecoat. They were all the rage at the time.

In 1961 my boyfriend bought me a white plastic handbag for my birthday. It was hideous, made me feel about fifty years old, but I had to cart it around just to please him. Then, thank god, leather shoulder bags came in and we could all ditch those awful handbags.

In the early sixties you bought your shoes – white sling-backs, with kitten heels – from Lilley & Skinner or Freeman, Hardy & Willis, and they cost 39/11, 49/11 or 59/11. There was a huge difference, depending on what you paid: 59/11 was really for best.

Do you remember those circular wicker baskets girls used to carry? They were like wicker hammocks. They went with the beehive, the sugared petticoat, the stiletto heels where the leather had worn off and the silver showed through, and lots of eye make-up.

I can remember when striped socks were supposed to be in. I got red and white striped socks, and I went to a school dance thinking I'm bound to crack it here, I've got these amazing socks. But of course no one could see them. I went around tapping people on the shoulder and lifting my trouser leg and saying, "Have you seen my socks?"

We'd spend all week working out what we'd wear at the dance hall. These were the days before jeans came in. For one dance, I wore a navy blue Marks & Spencer pleated terylene skirt, a thin pink wool round-necked jumper and a navy blue Orlon cardigan. I thought I was It. My friend was more arty-looking, because she was doing art: it rubs off. She was wearing a John Lennon cap.

Until about 1963, the casual gear we were expected to wear at boarding school consisted of a cravat and a Harris tweed jacket, then it suddenly changed to a roll-necked sweater, donkey jacket and desert boots.

Beatniks

I had an older brother at university when I was thirteen in 1960, and he would bring all these wonderful, exotic women home with him at the weekends. They wore black clothes and were going to become lawyers and doctors and so on. They were incredible role models to have; I was always ahead of my contemporaries because of them.

I desperately wanted to become a rebel, a beatnik, so I wouldn't have this grammar-school, middle-class girl image any more. I wore a lot of make-up, grew my hair long, wore jeans with bells on the ends and floppy sweaters – the whole beatnik trip, superficially. It's amazing to look back and realize how innocent it really was. Only a coffee bar, no purple hearts even. And how fantastically evil I thought it was.

I was always in complete awe of the beatniks. They were that much older than us, and seemed so much more sophisticated and intellectual, being into jazz and Sartre and Kerouac. I never dared to join them or be like them. But when the hippie movement came along I felt, yes, this is mine, and embraced it as much as I could.

I remember the coffee bars of Soho and around that area, central London. The first venue I ever went to was one of those folk places, full of people with beards and unkempt clothes, wearing berets, carrying folders of their artwork, having poetry readings.

We began going to folk clubs to hear the ideas of the beatniks. Dylan happened at that time and I got carried away just to hear the sound of his voice: the rasp, the wail, and the comments about war and peace; going to New York, Greenwich Village, coffee bars. That was the world I wanted.

The coffee bar in Stratford-on-Avon where I went to live in 1963, was called the Pit and was in at the beginning of the 'beat' circuit: St Ives, Brighton, Folkestone or Stratford, were the places where the beat with his bedroll and his newfound philosophy temporarily landed. The Acropolis in Folkestone was where you saw all these people wearing bleached jeans.

Beatnik men put on Dylan's 'man of constant sorrow' style, pretended to a depth of despair they couldn't really know, and it was a great turn-on. I used to think, when I was seventeen, that only men could really feel deep, philosophical sorrow. I used to fancy the moody type—all that angst and pain.

I went through a beatnik stage, via the San Francisco poets. I even had a record of Jack Kerouac reading his poetry with a piano background. On the Road was the bible.

My first boyfriend had been a chorister in the church I attended. Then the next time I saw him I nearly fell off my bench outside the pub, because he'd grown his hair, and he had a beard, and he smoked reefers and drank red wine straight from the bottle. He took me to a party; I went to C&A and bought a black cocktail frock with a lacy collar, so I looked like a deb and he looked really Bohemian, and we marched off to this party clutching two litre bottles of red wine, both of which he drank.

Mods and rockers

Mods were essentially from London and the South-East; everywhere else was a different world. We were followers of fashion. We used to go to the Ricki Tik clubs in Guildford and Windsor to see bands like Georgie Fame and the Blue Flames, R&B-type bands. We never ate anything, because we lived on purple hearts, a mixture of amphetamine and barbiturates. You had to have a Lambretta GT 200, with a flat side, or a Vespa GS 160 with a more bulbous back. You had to have lots of fur all over it: fox tails, and fur down the sides.

If you were on a GT 200 you had to have a pillion passenger, leaning right back with their arms folded. Their function in life was to gesticulate wildly when you went past a rocker café like the Ace on the North Circular Road or the Manor café at Blackwater. Then the rockers would all jump on their bikes and chase you. One friend used to have this spray can, I don't know what it was, hair spray or whatever, but it was very inflammable. The pillion passenger used to squirt it into the exhaust of the scooter and get this huge flame-thrower coming out the back.

Be as free as a bird, Leggy girl

Just slip into Berkshire pantie stockings and show the world a lovely leggy suspender-free leg . . . then walk free. Prices from 12/11 - 18/11.

in pantie stockings

BERKSHIRE B

KINK THINK: THIS 'TERYLENE' IS SMOOTH

'Smooth,' said Dave of the Kink when he saw Ina in her 'Terylen suit. 'Still smooth,' they both sa a dozen pictures later–after lots of sitting, kneeling, curling-up actio But then 'Terylene' has never crushed, never needed ironing after washin

TWIGGY LAWSON

Twiggy was launched at age 15 in the Daily Express *by Deirdre McSharry with Barry Lategan's photograph – with mod haircut and thick black eyelashes – and the headline 'This is the face of 1966.'*

"I was a mod – you were either a mod or a rocker – and the mods' bible was *Ready, Steady, Go.* You just didn't miss it. I can remember the excitement on Friday afternoons, coming home from school, because this was *Ready, Steady, Go* night – 'the weekend starts here' – yeah! Mods changed their clothes style almost every week, which was difficult, as I was a young (13–15-year-old) schoolgirl and Mum and Dad couldn't afford to keep buying me things. But luckily I could sew and would copy the clothes I'd seen on the older girls. Some of the 'must have' items I remember were brown Hush Puppy shoes (can you imagine, on the end of my skinny legs!), grey calf-length pleated skirt and a navy-blue nylon mac – an absolute must, even in winter. We'd freeze to death, but we were *in*."

...DAYS I'LL REMEMBER...

Rockers were essentially working class, because they came out of Teds in the fifties. They hated fashion; they were stuck in a time warp from the fifties. Their hairstyle was always the same, a greasy ducktail with Brylcreme. They were into drink and leathers, they liked Elvis and they went to places like the Agincourt ballroom in Camberley. They liked greasy food, cafés with juke boxes. And every rocker wanted to own something like a Triumph or a Norton 650. They were always aggressive. Once I was in a rocker café and one of them said to me, 'You eyein' up my bird?' I said, no; he said, 'You sayin' she's ugly?'

As a rocker you could have whole conversations just in letters and figures, such as:

'That a DBD 34?'

'DB 32.'

'With the double-R T2 box?'

'Yep.'

'Does that have the GP carb, then?'

'Nope – 10TT9. Your bike that T120?'

'Sort of – it started out a T110, but I gave it a Bonnie 9-stud head, twin Monoblocs, 10 to 1 pistons, ES3142 cams...'

And so on. If the bike was respected, so were you, generally, and I never saw much in the way of trouble. The loyal girls from the pillions – also in black leather and jeans and boots, usually with long blonde hair – sat around faithfully, saying very little indeed (you should have heard them on 'Terry' and 'Leader of the Pack', though) until it was time to follow their bloke out, wait for him to fire up the bike, and climb on the back again. Then off.

...into the sixties

I had skirts that stuck out with net underneath; a hangover from the fifties. But that changed with the Beatles, and also when Britain became a bit more European. We started to wear darker clothes. I remember being very proud of an outfit that consisted of a grey skinny-rib, a grey flannel skirt, really nice brown suede clumpy shoes –

because suddenly clumpy shoes came in, things you could walk in instead of horrible pointy things that you couldn't walk in. All my clothes became moody, beatnik style: black, grey, brown, how French girls dressed.

You could wear minis, or long skirts. There was suddenly much more flexibility. You could wear Courrèges or Mary Quant-style geometrics, sharp and neat and plain, or hippie-style things. There was a huge variety. I got my Courrèges-style boots from Russell & Bromley. Peter Robinson, Top Shop and Miss Selfridge started up.

Black polo-necked jumpers were totally in when the Beatles came in. You had to have one.

I remember feeling very marked out being the only girl in town with a Beatle jacket. It was in black suede and I bought it with my first Saturday morning job earnings, along with my first pair of black, knee-length 'kinky' boots.

My two best friends and I all had PVC macs, red, yellow and blue. And we each got a fur-trimmed bonnet.

Levi's were 32/6 or 37/6, one pound seventeen and six, and you could buy a belt for five shillings. You had to sit in the bath until they shrank, and copious amounts of dye came out – the bath was left dark blue.

I was going down to London to meet a pop singer for a date so I sewed along the seams of my jeans when they were on, to make drainpipes. I couldn't get in or out of them: they were completely skin tight. I didn't go to the toilet all evening – I couldn't. But when we went to a hotel to spend the night I had to unpick the seams to get undressed. I hadn't

taken a needle and thread to sew them up again, so the next morning they were a mess. He had to buy me a dress so we could go to his concert.

I wore so much eye make-up. Tons of dark brown eye shadow, eyeliner drawn all around, false eyelashes on top and painted eyelashes below, like Julie Driscoll. I sashayed into the student union one day and a (male) friend said, 'Hello, walk into a door did you?'

I used to buy fashion magazines more for wishful thinking than anything, and people like David Bailey changed the look completely. Clever, arty photography came in, making fashion more accessible. Twiggy and the Shrimp looked like normal people instead of haughty, upper-class clothes horses. They were ordinary girls from the suburbs; they were young, they were like us. It meant we could all aspire to interesting things. The world opened up. It was a very exciting time.

My friend went to London and came back to Wales wearing white boots with cut-outs, like the Courrèges ones, and masses of eye make-up, including false eyelashes and painted-on eyelashes underneath, and white lipstick. I thought she looked fantastic. I went to London, too, and bought myself a white PVC mac with black buttons from Miss Selfridge. Everyone asked me where my crossing sign was because I looked like a lollipop lady.

I remember big clip-on plastic earrings, Paco Rabanne style. I bought loads of them, mostly from Woolworths. Those and chain belts, and handbags with chain straps.

We all wanted to look like the girls the Beatles went out with – Patti Boyd, Jane Asher.

Hair

Everybody went out with their hair backcombed and frizzed and lacquered, and I remember the first person we saw who had a Mary Quant hairdo. It was dead straight, with a fringe, and came under her chin in a bob. We were amazed, especially when her hair moved when she danced. We'd spend all day getting ready to go out on Saturday night – there were girls who went shopping on Saturday mornings with rollers in their hair. We never stooped to that. When we'd finished backcombing we'd spray with this cheap lacquer that meant your hair was totally stiff and solid. So when we saw all the lads looking at this girl whose hair moved when she danced, we thought, maybe we should be doing something like that instead of all this ridiculous backcombing.

'Flick-ups' were a disastrous hairstyle for those of us with dead straight hair. You had to spend all night in agony with those plastic rollers with spikes making sleep almost impossible, and in the morning you'd find that one piece of hair flicked up more – or less – than the others. Then if

there was any moisture in the air whatsoever (which there always was) the whole lot would be drooping down, straight as a dye, by the time you got to the corner of your street – or, worse, *one* side was. Why we thought flick-ups were the thing I'll never know, because it's a very unnatural thing for hair to do, isn't it? It was such a relief when Sandy Shaw and Cathy McGowan came along and made straight hair okay.

The Beatle haircut was actually long-haired and bold then. They did create a whole new style.

When my hair got below my ears, I was thrashed and dragged over to the barber's for a pudding basin by my father. I didn't speak to him again for two years. Whenever he walked into a room, I walked out.

My friend Marion went to Vidal Sassoon's in London one weekend and had her hair cut into this brilliant geometric shape.

I had my hair cut by Vidal Sassoon himself, and I remember coming out of the salon and thinking, God, I look just like everybody else. You were just churned out.

I used to get into heaps of trouble about my hair. Teachers took it upon themselves to be hair monitors – or rather, hair dictators. You know: 'You can't play for the first eleven at football if you don't get your bloody hair cut.' But as long as I didn't look square, I didn't really mind. You had to have your hair a *little* bit long, otherwise you were branded as square, or weird.

Viva Biba!

We lived in a flat in Kensington Church Street, near a beautiful grocer's shop, which eventually became the new Biba. I used to use the grocer's, which had marble slabs and wonderful old characters in starched white aprons. We lived a few doors up, in a cul-de-sac called Holland Place Chambers. Ezra Pound had a flat on the top floor, and the Moody Blues started from there. So you'd see this old van parked on the pavement in this tiny cul-de-sac, with *the Moody Blues* written all over it in wonderful psychedelic lettering. Then one day the grocer's shop closed down and it was converted into an amazing clothes shop.

When boutiques like Biba opened you felt as though the whole world had opened up, too. You had to have long, straight hair, and big sooty eyes, and pale lipstick. That was Biba.

I used to go to Biba when it was in Abingdon Road, Kensington. It was like a temple. Because I was a single mother I didn't have a lot of money, so I'd buy things like beads.

My sister took me to Biba just after it opened. It was such an exotic place. Barbara Hulanicki would sit and sew up the hem for you herself, once you'd bought a dress. My sister bought a beautiful black dress with lace on the bottoms of the sleeves. My first Biba dress was an orange patterned mini. I felt so sophisticated and stylish when I wore it in Manchester – it was from the trendiest London boutique, after all.

BARBARA HULANICKI

Barbara Hulanicki was the founder of and genius behind Biba.

"One of my marvellous moments was the first time one of our mail order things just took off. It was 1963 and I designed a little gingham shift dress with keyhole at the back and matching kerchief. The offer was splashed across half a page of the *Daily Mirror*. We had a mail order address in Oxford Street, and normally we got about two or three hundred orders. We drove to Oxford Street and my husband Fitz went to get the mail – and he came round the corner and he was dragging three SACKS of mail, his face a beaming moon. We had 17,000 orders for that dress, all in 25-shilling postal orders. Fitz took them to Barclays Bank and they said, 'Sorry, we're not accepting this.' So he went round to the Nat West and we stayed with them for ever more.

That little gingham dress was like winning the lottery – it meant we'd got it right. I'd been doing fashion illustration before that, and I had to draw the dreadful clothes available then: terrible shapes, badly cut, unwearable. The next year, 1964, we opened our first Biba shop in Kensington, and two years later the bigger Biba in Church Street. We had a whole load of jersey dresses arrive that hadn't been properly stretched first and we were horrified to see the skirts were crotch-high. But the girls flocked in and leapt on them – we couldn't believe it – and we never looked back."

...DAYS I'LL REMEMBER...

I remember my mother saying, when I left school, that I should always buy good quality, timeless clothes like classic tweed skirts, Pringle sweaters and so on. But times had changed, and this kind of advice was completely irrelevant. I mean, I was wearing Biba paper dresses. You bought them for three quid and wore them two or three times – maybe even once, depending on what you spilt on them – then tossed them out. I had a lovely pink one; I was sorry it was paper, actually, because I could have kept it for ever. You had to wear a petticoat underneath, and they were pretty uncomfortable, and you couldn't wash them, of course, but they looked great.

I had a lilac Dr Zhivago coat from Biba, with black frogging. I thought I was the bee's knees. It hid everything too, which was very useful.

In the mid-sixties, the whole of West London was seething with beautiful people. Everyone had heard of Biba by then, and we thought, why don't we open one in Birmingham? So we did. We'd go into Biba every week and see what fashions were in. We had to adapt them all for the Birmingham market, because they hadn't even seen their knees at that stage, let alone their crotches. We had to introduce tights, because they were worried about people seeing their underwear. It was called The Alley, and all the Birmingham girls would bring their mothers and boyfriends with them every Saturday. We had music, and magazines, and places for people to sit. It was a complete breakthrough in terms of shopping; it was a happening, Birmingham's first boutique. We held an outdoor fashion parade in the Bullring in

1966, with music and posters and razzamatazz, and it was such a new thing to do.

One garment I remember, when Barbara Hulanicki went into longer stuff, you had a hook-y thing that came over your finger, like a ring. Long sleeves, with this V at the end hooked onto your middle finger. That was so elegant.

There were tops and dresses that you didn't have to wear a bra under. That was quite a breakthrough: we'd only just come out of the era of whirlpool bras.

For the first time, people didn't want expensive clothes that would last a long time. They wanted something fashionable that would last

a couple of weeks, then they'd move on and buy something else. Colour, instant fashion, being trendy.

PATRICIA HODGE

Patricia Hodge is a well-known actress.
"The early sixties to me meant space travel (so futuristic) and *Honey* magazine (so trendy) and having a portable radio with a shoulder strap and listening to Carole King's 'It Might As Well Rain Until September'. I had a hipster skirt from Neatawear, and at school we turned our blazers inside out and used our lacrosse sticks as guitars to copy the Fab Four. We also ran 'the Stork Stakes', a sweepstake on the crop of Royal babies born in 1964, guessing which sex they would be and what they would be named.

As the sixties progressed our hipsters got lower and lower and I wore a mini-skirt when I went for a teaching job, causing a great stir among the children. I remember loving Joan Baez (we all learnt the guitar) and painting extra eyelashes on our lower lids, and feeling out of it if you hadn't got long blonde hair. The arrival of boutiques, Biba and Mary Quant's Bazaar: suddenly there were fashions especially for young people. And finally, discovering Badedas!"

...DAYS I'LL REMEMBER...

Mini skirts

We were wearing mini skirts in Britain long before anyone else was. Jean Shrimpton may have caused a big sensation in Australia when she wore her mini to the Melbourne Cup in 1965, but I'd already caused a minor sensation in Paris that year. We were so used to them that we forgot how extraordinary people elsewhere found it, seeing young girls wearing strips of material that scarcely covered their bums.

Mini-dresses in hot summer weather were quite something. Boys used to say the girls were coming out in their flowery knickers on the first day of warm weather. I enjoyed the 'flasher' feeling, I loved wearing those short, revealing dresses.

I was at a party in New York early in 1966 and at one stage I was surrounded by men, who were trying to measure how far up from my knees my skirt came. I think it was about four and a half inches. Some of the older guys were just about apoplectic. Luckily I was there with my parents, otherwise I probably wouldn't be here to tell the tale.

My sister gave me a fantastic Indian mirror-patterned jacket in 1966. I wore it as a mini dress, and it only just covered my bum. It had sleeves, so you couldn't raise your arms when you wore it, because if you did, you'd be arrested.

Mini skirts were great fun. But we kept hearing about girls who wore mini skirts in the winter getting an extra layer of fat on their thighs, to compensate for the cold. This was a bit alarming, and may have prompted maxi coats, do you remember them? So you wore your micro mini skirt, with tights, and over it a huge maxi coat to keep warm. And, of course, boots.

Cool

In 1966, in Carnaby Street, I bought a blue short-sleeved shirt with epaulettes and a button-down collar, pale blue denim slacks, denim-y canvas shoes and a blue peaked cap. I got clip-on sunglasses for over my glasses. Then I bought *Steppenwolf*. So you bought all this stuff and you just knew you were now *it*. Everything's going to change, everything's going to be fine. I went to Hampstead Heath, it was a sunny day, and I remember sitting there waiting for it all to happen, waiting to be transported off into this world of models and fashion photographers and pop stars.

You conned yourself that by wearing your black PVC raincoat and your sunglasses, you were part of the revolution.

I remember walking through Kensington Market and seeing a pair of beautiful mustard yellow ankle boots, with platform soles and very high heels. I bought them for my boyfriend, and he tottered around wearing them with a pair of purple and grey striped loons, a shirt with a huge collar you had to put those stiffeners in, and a pink and white PVC mac. I thought he looked fantastic.

With my first grant cheque at university I bought a fabulous 'fun fur' – a white, grey and black rabbitskin coat – and a pair of beige leather knee-high lace-up boots. Wearing those, with a mini dress, I felt like a film star. Until one night when I got horribly drunk at the Thursday night dance and peed in the boots on the way home. They were never quite the same after that. I became known as 'Piss in Boots'.

Mr Fish did sharp suits, and there were chains of shops like Lord John that did men's fashion. Half of the shops in Carnaby Street were men's shops.

I went to Take Six in Wardour Street and bought a kind of waisted donkey jacket and flared trousers so big that your shoes disappeared. I used to shop at Lawrence Corner, the Army surplus place. They had the best loons in the world, proper ex-sailor's trousers that they dyed in psychedelic colours, and other bits of naval kit like square-necked shirts and sweaters.

You bought ridiculously-shaped ties, like kipper ties, because they were halfway between being a hippie and being square. You wore shirts with collars that came up almost as high as Regency collars and down to your nipples. I remember experimenting with crimson jeans

and things like that: black jeans, crimson velvet flares, pink shirts.

I outgrew my parents' image of me as the nice daughter, the educated, well-mannered girl, who some day would make some nice man a nice wife. I started to get scruffier. Baggy jeans and loose, sloppy T-shirts with no bra underneath. Straggly hair. Long skirts that

swept the ground. Dun colours. I knew that I was rebelling against looking 'pretty'. The one thing I did not want to look in those days was 'bourgeois'. To look bourgeois was the biggest sin.

Hippies

The hippie movement was from *my* generation. I desperately wanted to be one, but I never quite made it because you had to be either terribly rich or a complete drop-out. I ended up being a sort of weekend hippie, wearing long floaty things, even occasionally flowers in my hair, but going to lectures and doing the conventional thing. And always feeling slightly self-conscious about going around in hippie gear; a bit of a fraud.

We just laughed at people who took the whole hippie thing too seriously. People who dressed up in things that looked like sheets and togas, and went around claiming to have seen UFOs and saying 'oh *man!*' all the time.

In the summer of 1967 there were flowers-in-their-hair hippies in Brighton. I put on my jeans, with my black satin shirt, long silk scarves, and every single string of beads I could find. With my hair loose, I walked through Brighton.

Haight-Ashbury was a shock and a disappointment. There were no flowers, or peace, or love. This was 1968, and the streets were tatty, the people looked dead. Too many wasted addicts hanging around; kids with their eyes glazed over and their faces old.

Music

After clothes and hair, music was the defining mantra of the sixties. If our parents had been horrified by Bill Haley and Elvis Presley in the fifties, they nearly had seizures when they heard the Rolling Stones, Them, even the Beatles. And later on, music became the essential background to dope-smoking. The music was ours, not theirs. The music was everything. Although you weren't actually creating the music, there was an incredible feeling of ownership.

I kept a list of my favourite records, starting in September 1959 with 'My Wish Come True' by Elvis Presley, followed by 'Three Bells' by The Browns and 'Keep it Up' by Dee Clark. The idea was to compile my top 1,000, but although I did keep it up diligently for years I only ever got to number 970, which was 'Somewhere in the Night' by Brian Hyland, listed in May 1963. I still have the yellowing pages, more sticky tape than paper, but still legible.

I used to buy singles in the very early sixties, when I could afford them. Michael Holiday, Tommy Steele. I remember a friend suggesting I go to Woolworth's and buy a cover version, Embassy Records, half the price of the real thing, and you just didn't do that. If I wanted Ruby Murray I wanted the *real* Ruby Murray.

MAUREEN CLEAVE

Journalist Maureen Cleave wrote a column in the Evening Standard *in the early 1960s which introduced all the new pop stars.*

"My column was called (oh shame) 'Disc Date', when the *Standard* was one of the first papers to print stories about what was still in inverted commas everywhere else – 'pop' music, as distinct from real music which was made by Perry Como.

I remember Tommy Steele telling me that until he was famous he had never been to the West End, even though the bus that ran outside his home in Bermondsey said 'Piccadilly'. Terence Stamp, who'd earned a fortune as a lorry driver since the age of 17, complained to me in 1963 that there was nothing to spend money on, nowhere to go, nothing to do. 'Nowhere to take girls, nowhere to sit down in England. But the working classes are banging on a door that's no longer closed. People like me, we're moderns. We work hard and we play hard. We have no class and no prejudice. We're the new swinging Englishmen.' Prophetic words. A week later I interviewed the Beatles. They were, I said, a vocal instrument group whose physical appearance inspired frenzy. Their haircuts I described as French. 'The only thing I'm afraid of,' said John Lennon, 'is growing old. They get old and they've missed it somehow.' Henceforth we had a youth culture."

...DAYS I'LL REMEMBER...

I was brought up to think that pop was vulgar; well, of course, vulgar was our culture, so I liked Adam Faith, and Gerry and the Pacemakers.

At school, there was a cachet about liking and having really obscure blues records. I'd seek out records by people like Blind Lemon Jefferson and Big Bill Broonzy of course, but also recordings made by the Lomax brothers of songs of the workers, recorded in the factories, songs of railway workers and hobos.

My parents bought me a Dansette record player when I was sixteen, and I left the arm off to play the latest 45 hit over and over again at full volume. They hardly ever complained, so I'm now very lenient with my own children when they play music loudly.

We didn't have sound systems in the early sixties like we have now. You were lucky if there was a record player in the house. Then, when we all really got into rock music, stereos became cult status items, especially among blokes: who had the biggest speakers, the most expensive turntable, the most records.

When I went to Oxford in 1963 there were a couple of American Rhodes scholars down the corridor, both I thought fantastically sophisticated, talking about jazz and playing Frank Sinatra loudly. That was just about the coolest thing going.

I had an almost total obsession with pop music. I would play records all the time. You'd go and buy a record – a little 45 rpm, maybe one a fortnight – and you'd just play it over and over. 'Halfway to Paradise', things like that.

Second-hand record shops started selling ex-juke-box records; instead of paying 6/10d a record, you could get one for a shilling. They had no middle, and they were all unbelievably warped, but if you could put up with that it meant that you could have loads of records every week.

I liked mod music, bands like The Who, and rhythm and blues. But I also liked jazz. Jazz was big around Hampstead, both traditional and modern, and we had a jazz club at Wood Green every Sunday. It was only half a crown or something. Some of the jazz bands turned into rhythm and blues bands later on, such as Mike Cotton. Eric Clapton used to come along regularly, with John Mayall, to the Tuesday night rhythm and blues nights.

The coming of the Beatles

I had this ridiculous feeling of superiority about the Beatles. My brother went to university in Liverpool in 1961, and he began writing home about a group he used to see called the Beatles in a club called the Cavern, and I told my schoolfriends about it. So when they made a record, I could have this pretence of knowing all about it, because I'd heard of them first. I really had street cred about that.

One afternoon in late November 1962, my friend and I used the fog as an excuse to rush home and skip the hellish after-school ballroom dancing class with the local boys' grammar school because there was a new group going to be on TV for the first time. Somebody, the day before, had brought their single into school. It was

'Love Me Do', they were the Beatles, and we were ready to break out – with their help.

When the Beatles first came out singing 'Love Me Do', I thought they were a barber shop quartet. They sounded like the Mike Samms Singers or somebody like that. I couldn't believe it when they became so popular.

I thought the Beatles were light years ahead of everyone else, and I think they changed the world.

I remember *Revolver* coming out, and we all took it very seriously: it wasn't just the Beatles doing their thing, it was educated parents sitting down and talking about it with us, and giving us the notion that what we did was important. Then *The Times* did that piece on the Beatles, and all the other groups paled into insignificance.

Everybody wanted to be Liverpudlian. I was from Birmingham, and we missed out completely in the pop music stakes. Steve Winwood was the only Brummie who made the scene, just about. Whenever I visited my friend in Liverpool it was like going to Mecca.

Dylan

I remember walking down a street in Soho one lunch hour and hearing 'The Times They Are A-'Changin' coming out of a record shop, and literally stopping in the street, transfixed. Then I went into the shop and asked if I could listen to it, which you could in those days, in a little booth. And I thought, 'Wow!' I bought it and took it home and listened to it endlessly in my bedsit, and was totally blown away.

I *loved* Dylan. I didn't understand half the words to his songs (it was years before I realized he was singing 'that's not where it's at' on 'Positively Fourth Street'), but that didn't matter. He was so strange, so cerebral, so different from all the pop stuff. Bohemian and interesting and *deep*.

It was the beginning of message songs. You actually had to listen to the words, because they were all saying something.

'Like a Rolling Stone' seemed to be Bob Dylan's message to nice bourgeois girls desperate to get out. We sat in my bedroom, half a dozen girls who'd come through the grammar school mill, and Dylan's song had a powerful effect. Creating that feeling of independence, of wanting to fly like a bird. Now it was time to leave home.

147

Psychedelia

Some of that 'psychedelic' music practically gave you a high without any illegal substances being involved at all. A sort of op art for the brain.

A friend used to really get into Pink Floyd's 'Set the Controls for the Heart of the Sun' when he was stoned. He'd lie there, eyes closed, and shout 'Fire retros!' just before the climax.

I remember my older sister coming home with a poster of Che Guevara, then a poster of Eric Clapton from Cream. Listening to her records of the Who. The first record I bought was 'Substitute' from Boots the Chemist; you could go to the chemist and buy all these covers of popular songs by other people.

99 EXPECTING TO FLY — BUFFALO SPRINGFIELD

HUNTER DAVIES

Hunter Davies was working on the 'Atticus' column of The Sunday Times *in 1967 when he met the Beatles and became their authorized biographer.*

"The thing that sums up the sixties for me is being given a reefer by Ringo, taking it home, closing the curtains, putting the phone off the hook, lighting up. Nothing happened, so after half an hour we opened the phone, put the curtains on the hook and got back to work. At the time, you see, nothing seemed to be happening. That was just like the sixties for me. At the time, it all seemed pretty ordinary; how it was, how it would always be. Only now, looking back, do I realize it was the most extraordinary decade."

...DAYS I'LL REMEMBER...

When you were with your girlfriend, there were certain songs that were basically songs for sex. Things like 'The End' by the Doors.

My favourite of all sixties bands was Them. They were fantastic live, unlike many bands of the time. I saw them at the Astoria, Finsbury Park.

The music was suddenly much more exciting. The oldies hated it, so there must have been something good there. It's endured, hasn't it; it's stood the test of time. Still being played, and bought by young people, thirty-forty years on. Cream, Led Zeppelin, all the stuff we baby boomers were brought up on.

JOANNA LUMLEY

Joanna Lumley was a model in the sixties, before finding acting fame in 'The New Avengers' in the seventies and eternal glory as Patsy in 'Absolutely Fabulous' in the nineties.

"It was 1964. Earl's Court Road was then still two-way – a hot summer's evening, and instead of the rush hour an extraordinary silence and emptiness had descended on London, on England, on Britain. I came out of the tube station and hurried down the street to my aunt's flat, where I was staying while I did my Lucie Clayton course in modelling. No one to be seen by the flower-stall, the newspaper stand. If I sprinted I would get there in time. The nation held its breath because that evening the four Beatles, all the Fab Four, were appearing live on *Juke Box Jury*: John, Paul, George and Ringo being cool, hip, smart, lippy, charming and funny. It was very heaven to be alive."

...DAYS I'LL REMEMBER...

I bought *Cheap Thrills* as soon as it became available. Janis Joplin meant a lot to me. She knew what it meant to be a gutsy, ballsy girl, to want to do everything the boys did, and then to suffer because she wasn't feminine enough. She knew all about those pent-up feelings, about the claustrophobia that comes from a straight upbringing.

Radio

Before the broadcasting honchos cottoned on to the fact that the teenage audience was the way of the future, there was very little for us to listen to. We were stuck with our parents singing along to 'Sing Something Simple', the BBC Light Orchestra and 'The Billy Cotton Band Show'. So who can forget the thrill of tuning in to Radio Luxembourg in those rock-famished days and hearing all the pop songs we'd ever desired? Even if the reception was lousy, the songs were faded out after a minute or so, and every three nanoseconds there'd be an ad for Horace Batchelor and his infallible gambling schemes based at Keynsham, spelled K-E-Y-N-S-H-A-M, near Bristol.

We'd all take the mickey out of the Horace Batchelor ad at school, saying, 'Keynsham, I'll spell that again: T-H-A-T.'

You begged for a transistor radio for Christmas, and you sat in your room and listened to Radio Luxembourg. My parents thought it was dreadful because it was commercial and played nothing but pop music, but I loved it. It was all very exciting. Music began to dominate everything, and became a talking point for teenagers.

I remember lying in the dark, listening to Radio Luxembourg, and feeling as though I suddenly belonged to a worldwide conspiracy, a movement. People everywhere were listening to the same thing, in the same way. All of a sudden, *life* was beginning.

My first awareness of people like Cliff Richard, and the fact that there were pop songs going on, was gathered around a horrible little radio set in the House library of an English public school on Sunday afternoons, listening to *Pick of the Pops*. I especially remember it as a winter scenario, with steam on the windows and lots of little boys with boils on their faces, crowding around a hissing gas fire trying to toast their crumpets, listening to Alan Freeman.

When I was about fifteen I bought myself a tape recorder, but of course I had to record off this big old radio we had, sticking a microphone in front of it. I've got loads of recordings with a canary singing its heart out in the background.

The pirate stations were such a relief because they played the same stuff as Radio Luxembourg but seemed to have a much better broadcasting facility. So for the first time you could actually hear the music properly. The whole business of them being outlawed and hounded was ludicrous; I mean, what were they doing that was so heinous? It was an early instance of 'Big Brother' meddling in *our* affairs.

Pirate radio stations were so important. We just had to listen to Radio Caroline, it was so different from everything else that had ever been on the radio. The music they played was fantastic, the DJs were fantastic, including Kenny Everett. The blurb between the records was really good. I remember lying on a rug in the garden listening to Radio Caroline on a little transistor radio and revising my History A-level notes with my friend.

Concerts

A few of us girls went to the Beatles concert in Cheltenham and they got us all screaming. I don't remember much about the concert, just the noise. Everyone screamed. It was rather like being on the Big Wheel. When that goes hurtling down, out of control, you have to scream to release yourself. Screaming, hysteria, knicker wetting – they're all related.

I remember queuing up to see the Searchers at my local town hall, but I didn't really like going to concerts because everybody screamed. It was the most mindless thing. You couldn't hear the music, and you just got deafened. So I stuck to my record collection.

I went to the Beatles concert at the Wigan Ritz, with Gene Pitney and Mary Wells also on the bill. I wore a pencil-slim skirt and I spent the whole time

RADIO CAROLINE...

on Saturday at 12.45-1 p.m.,

RADIO LONDON...

on Saturday at 11.45 a.m.-12 noon.

screaming. I have no idea what they sang, but I remember the camaraderie of everyone there. We were all so happy to be there, part of a huge party.

I was sitting close to the front at the Beatles concert in Hull, and I never heard a single note. It was a continuous, deafening cacophony of screaming. To keep up that very high-pitched and very loud screaming for that long – it was well over an hour – is amazing. If you really fixed your eyes on the stage, you thought you knew which one was singing. I was obsessed with the Beatles so I was very disappointed by this concert, because I'd really like to have heard them.

When I was seventeen, in 1964, my friend and I got tickets to the Mad Mod Ball at Wembley where the Stones were playing, stuck out on a platform in the centre of the

★

THE
BEATLES

★

★

WINTER
GARDENS
MARGATE

★

Programme Sixpence

stadium. We had dancing tickets, which meant we could get really close. I doubt if the Stones ever played so near their audience again. I can remember their terrified faces, when they were trying to get off the stage, surrounded by the heaving, maniacal, screaming mob.

The sixties began for me when I discovered the Rolling Stones. I hated the teachers at school, I hated

BOOKENDS/SIMON & GARFUNKEL

the most bizarre event. It was just after Brian Jones had died, and the thing that sticks out in my memory is Mick Jagger opening up the box of butterflies after reading the Shelley poem 'Adonais'. The butterflies had been kept in the box too long. They flew up six or seven feet above the stage, then the Stones went into their next song – which I think was '(I Can't Get No) Satisfaction' – and suddenly the butterflies all fluttered back down to the stage. They sat there quivering as Mick Jagger stomped around the stage, stomping all over these butterflies.

authority, so when the Rolling Stones appeared on the scene I was immediately attracted. I went to see them before they were famous, at Sophia Gardens in Cardiff in about 1964, just as they released 'Not Fade Away'. It was a dance hall, rather than a concert in a theatre. You could dance away and look up at Mick Jagger's knickers on the stage next to you, practically.

We went to the Simon and Garfunkel concert in Manchester in 1968, and I remember thinking it was just like listening to the records. They were phenomenal, better than the best group around.

A friend told me one day in 1969 that there was a gig coming up the following Sunday, and they needed extra stage crew, so I said I'd do it. And it was the big rock concert in Hyde Park, the Stones in the Park concert. So we did stage management there, and it was

Dance halls and clubs

The dances were so important. We used to go to the Embassy Ballroom in Wigan, which was huge, or to Bolton Palais. I got ten bob a week pocket money, and I had to buy a pair of stockings every week because they always laddered. Then you had to pay to get into the ballroom, get a drink of lemonade in there, and your bus fare there and back. That took care of the ten bob.

My main recollection of the Cavern is an absolutely unbelievable level of noise, and a strong smell of disinfectant. Every night they swabbed it out. But there were lots of clubs around Birkenhead then, with amazing people playing, not just the Beatles: Gerry and the Pacemakers, Billy J. Kramer. They'd play the local church halls, school dances and stuff.

Rory Storm and the Hurricanes; Wayne Fontana. Great music.

I used to go to all the mod music venues, I'd ride my Vespa to the Marquee Club up West

and to the Con Hall at Finchley. I wore Hush Puppies and PVC macs. I even wore a pork-pie hat for a while, it was my dad's. Discomfort didn't seem to matter. We'd go into these dance halls wearing parkas – army surplus stuff designed to keep people warm in the frozen wastes of Antarctica, and we'd wear them in rooms full of people. We wouldn't take them off, either.

Ronnie Scott's first club was a tiny place below a Chinese restaurant, down a fire staircase. It was very grungy, but it was a jazz club, with very exciting music: a tenor player called Tubby Hayes, a trumpet player called Jimmy Ducat, a keyboard player called Georgie Fame. Ronnie Scott had a

VALERIE GROVE

Valerie Grove started her Fleet Street career as a reporter on the Londoner's Diary of the Evening Standard *in the flower-power summer of 1967.*

"The first inkling I'd had that times were really changing was at school when Mr Oliver, the economics master, seized my copy of *Private Eye* – it was issue number 4, in 1962 – with Hugh Gaitskell on the cover, and after protesting 'How cruel to poor Mr Gaitskell!' he then read the whole thing through, sniggering and chortling. So satirizing politicians was OK! Then in 1966 the first Brook Advisory Clinic opened, including one in Cambridge. So going on the Pill was not just OK for students: it was almost obligatory. And in the summer of 1967, I was on the 'Londoner's Diary' and almost every day in London there was a happening or a love-in to cover. I sat at the feet of all four Beatles at the Hilton Hotel on the hot August night when they went to hear the Maharishi for the first time. And a bunch of Sloaney young things went and squatted in a grand old house once lived in by King George VI, at 144 Piccadilly. When I met these Arabellas and Jonathans and found that even they were calling this place 'a great crash-pad' I knew Bob Dylan was right, the sons and daughters were beyond their parents' commands. And I remember great swathes of colour: Indian caftans, mirror sequins and psychedelic prints, flower-power trouser suits and all the phantasmagoria of exuberantly coloured cottons and lace and seersucker. There has never been such a colourful world, before or since."

...DAYS I'LL REMEMBER...

when all the other musicians would finish their gigs and come over to Ronnie Scott's.

Folk was a big thing in the early sixties, but I didn't get involved in it myself. It was all a bit too earnest; they were too purist. They were the people who booed Dylan when he went electric.

I went to the UFO club in London, in Tottenham Court Road, where Soft Machine, Purple Gang, Pink Floyd played. I used to go with my older sister. Two groovy girls from my school used to go too, and when they saw me there my status shot up. I hadn't a clue what was going on there. I remember the smell of the place, the joss sticks; and there were a lot of pills around, not so much marijuana.

COMPLIMENTARY TICKET

LA PREMIÈRE DISCOTHEQUE FRANÇAISE
CARTE COMPLIMENTAIRE - FREIKARTE
COMPLENENTARIO DILLETE
BILIEPPO DI COMPLINTI

THE PURPLE PUSSYCAT

LONDON'S SWINGIEST DISCOTHEQUE

307 FINCHLEY ROAD N.W
ENTRANCE IN LITHOS RO

OPEN FROM EIGHT TILL LATE

Telephone: SWI 2801 and SWI 3

I went to the Arts Lab once but nothing happened. I thought, is this the counter-culture? And actually, it was.

London was having a ball in those years. There was a guy called Jim Haynes who ran the Arts Lab; leading liberationist of his day. He was wonderful fun. I used to go to the Arts Lab all the time. We didn't do very much; we lay around on mattresses and watched light shows and listened to strange music and felt incredibly psychedelic. We didn't drink much, and there were only modest amounts of drugs going on. We just lay about in heaps and thought it was the coolest thing in the world.

somewhat black sense of humour. He must have started on an absolute shoestring; I remember being there on nights when there'd be five or six other people – until midnight,

Fundraising concerts at the Roundhouse were always really good. And there was a club in Wardour Street where I first heard a band called King Crimson. Astonishing noise, strobe lights, mind-altering substances: it took me a while to recover. It was my first experience of that type of thing.

The Saturday night dances at the Student Union seemed to attract people like Manfred Mann, the Searchers, the Hollies; all the top groups came, we took it for granted. I'll never forget Jimi Hendrix. We got into the hall and it was so jam packed there was no room for a single extra body. We pushed our way along the back wall and eventually climbed on to a windowsill and stood there. On the other side was a three-storey drop. There was a waterfall coming down the wall from all the condensation, and all you could see in front of you was this sea of humanity. Then Hendrix came on, and you hadn't got a clue what he was singing or playing because there was just this *staggering* volume of noise, totally distorted. The loudest noise I've ever heard in my life.

The Animals came and played at one of our college balls. They were appallingly young and spotty, but nevertheless they looked far wilder and more mature and interesting than we all felt in our dinner jackets. Long John Baldry played at one ball; Francois Hardie sang at another.

Dancing

When the Liverpool sound was starting to happen, there was a lot of local energy around. Tennis clubs and church socials had a huge number of bands to call on, really good bands. It was great music to dance to. We were being taught foxtrots and waltzes at dancing lessons, but when we went to the dances it was completely different.

When it came out, the Twist was such an innovation. You knew you looked good doing it, and you knew your parents looked bloody stupid. They hadn't been able to jive, that was too energetic, but anyone could do the twist. But only we teenagers looked good.

I remember when 'Can't Buy Me Love' came out. We did our own jump jive. We used to jump ourselves silly. I remember, too, winning a competition for the Shake. I won a pound. We had so much energy.

We did The March of the Mods, with everybody in a line doing a set dance. Joe Loss and His Orchestra. The dance floor was sprung, and it would go up and down as we danced, very simple steps like the Shadows did.

There was a great, arm-twisting, gyrating style of dancing that came in with the Tamla Motown sound. We all did it, around 1966-67. Even guys who'd never danced before found they could do it, because it meshed so well with the music. The sound

and the movement were perfect together. And even better: you didn't need a partner. For the first time, you could just get out there on the dance floor and do your thing. End of wallflowers!

Television

I vividly remember slouching around in my parents' living room one boring Saturday afternoon when the very first *Dr Who* came on the TV – listening to that eerie theme music for the first time and getting goosebumps, and being mesmerized by the amazing idea of the Tardis and its journeyings. There were other great sci-fi programmes: *The Twilight Zone* and of course *Star Trek*.

My friend Elaine used to come round to my house on Saturday night and if we didn't have anything else planned we'd watch *Rawhide* on television with my mother. We watched a hell of a lot of *Rawhide*.

6.5 Special was still around at the beginning of the sixties. And *Juke Box Jury*. David Jacobs in the chair, and Pete Murray. In early 1960 Gracie Fields came out of retirement and recorded 'Jerusalem'. They played it on *Juke Box Jury*, and they had Gracie in that booth behind the panel, so the panellists couldn't see her. And of course they all said what an embarrassment it was; then she came out and they all had to smile gracefully and shake her hand.

I can remember my grandmother watching all the banal quiz shows, *Double Your Money, Take Your Pick,* and getting really involved. If somebody opened the box and it was a booby prize and she had been shouting at them to take the money, she would just go wild, crying 'I *knew* it was a booby!' She'd have a hankie stuffed in her mouth, she was so wound up.

I used to go for my school holidays to an aunt who lived in Weston-Super-Mare and ran a rigid sort of household, where the nearest we came to listening to popular music was *Music While You Work*. But at least there we had television, and as soon as *Ready, Steady, Go* and *Juke Box Jury* started I would get a little glimpse of what was happening. But the television for them served much more as sitting down with trolleys loaded with cheese and pickles and celery sticks to watch *Armchair Theatre*, which was absolutely wonderful drama. You remember them with absolute pleasure, and wonder why they don't happen now – I suppose because we're all too impatient, we've all seen too many zippy movies.

There were some great comedy shows. *Steptoe and Son, Hancock's Half-Hour, Morecambe and Wise.* And do you remember when every comedian had to have a catchphrase? Norman Vaughan with `swingin'!' and `dodgy', accompanied by thumbs up or thumbs down.

the sights and sounds

Cathy McGowan and *Ready, Steady, Go* were magic, compulsory viewing. Manfred Mann singing '5, 4, 3, 2, 1' was the theme music. I'll never forget that wonderful catch-cry 'The weekend starts here!', with the accompanying feeling of freedom, excitement and *youth*.

I didn't finish work in Tottenham until half-past five, and *Ready, Steady, Go* came on at six. It was incredibly tight for me to get back to Highgate in time to watch it, but I wasn't worth living with if I missed it. I remember one Friday night when the bus was caught in some traffic snarl-up in Crouch End, and I ran all the way home in four-minute-mile time, arriving, covered in sweat, just in time to crash into the front room as the show started. My parents thought I was crazy.

When I got to university in 1966 there was a television room in the basement of my hall of residence. I very much wanted to watch *Top of the Pops* and *Dr Who* but had a suspicion this would be regarded as desperately uncool. So that first week I didn't tell anyone where I was going and snuck quietly down the stairs to watch *Top of the Pops*. My progress was halted halfway

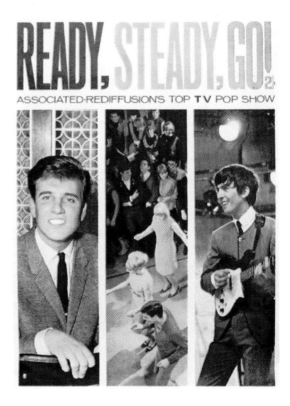

READY, STEADY, GO!

ASSOCIATED-REDIFFUSION'S TOP **TV** POP SHOW

TV TIMES
Mar 27 to Apr 2

ready steady goes live!
FRIDAY ... with CATHY McGOWAN

by the seething mass of humanity gathered to do just that. I learnt that you had to arrive at least half an hour earlier to guarantee a seat. Same with *Dr Who*, same with *Star Trek*. It was such a relief. In fact they were highlights of the week, all the more enjoyable because you were watching them with a couple of hundred others, shouting and whistling and groaning in unison. Not stuck in your parents' living room with only siblings for company and a big Disapproval vibe coming from elsewhere in the house.

Glamorous programmes like *The Avengers* came along, and bizarre stuff like *The Prisoner*. And great police dramas like *Z Cars*.

John Berger did a fantastic series called *Looking at Paintings*, where he got very ordinary people, people like my mum, on the telly to talk about a Rembrandt or something. It was watched by millions, and nobody thought 'this is above us' at all. It was the same with things like *Armchair Theatre*. There was no dumbing down. They did the whole of *The Age of Kings*, which we all watched.

AN PREMIO INTERNAZIONALE DEL FESTIVAL DI CANNES 1967

TRO-GOLDWYN-MAYER presenta una produzione **CARLO PONTI**

FILM DI **MICHELANGELO ANTONIONI**

BLOW-UP

VANESSA **REDGRAVE** DAVID **HEMMINGS** SARAH **MILES**

TECHNICOLOR

We didn't get colour television until the late sixties. The main impact was on televized football games: at last, you could tell which team was which.

Films, theatre, happenings

The quintessential movie about the sixties, the one that's about being inside and outside – and I felt all the way through the sixties that I was on the outside, but too close to the inside – was Antonioni's *Blow-Up*. I saw it one day and went back to see it again the next; it was *exactly* right.

I remember thinking how funny *Billy Liar* was when I read it at school. The film is one of my all-time favourites. Everybody was in love with Julie Christie. It painted a true picture of what life still really was like in the sixties. There still was an Establishment.

I've never felt comfortable watching something risqué with someone I think is going to disapprove. So I was always desperate to get my parents to bed so I could really enjoy *That Was The Week That Was*. If they stayed up I was excruciatingly embarrassed because on *TW3* they would do things like swear, which was terribly unusual then. It fitted my feelings and views; I didn't know about satire then, but its targets were the old fuddy-duddies I hated and I thought it was so funny. It was totally new, and a great experience – as long as you got your mum and dad to bed first.

This is Benjamin.

He's a little worried about his future.

THE GRADUATE

My first date with my future husband was going to a double bill of *A Taste of Honey* and *Saturday Night and Sunday Morning*. Great stuff. To our shock, when we emerged from the Raynes Park Rialto, his parents were coming out too. All the kitchen sink stuff was wonderful.

There was a sense of discovering something new that wasn't what we'd been taught. I remember thinking 'The Continentals' were really interesting; that they had something beyond Norman Wisdom and Benny Hill. They had Jean-Luc Godard.

There were only certain cinemas that you went to in the early sixties, and if it wasn't on at one of those art-house cinemas you didn't go.

Antonioni, Visconti, Alain Renais, Ingmar Bergman were all beginning to go into colour, because they'd all done black and white before and colour was for Hollywood. I remember Antonioni's first colour film was *The Red Desert* in 1964, and he was quite late. Some of those films were so violent and hideous, about the underbelly of Milano and things, but I thought they were wonderful. Oh, it's foreign, it's wonderful.

It was almost a shock when Hollywood started to make films about 'us': films like *The Graduate, Midnight Cowboy, Zabriski Point, Easy Rider*. I mean, none of us had actually hustled in Manhattan or blown up buildings in California or ridden Harleys through New Orleans, but at least these films weren't about sophisticated twenty-somethings living in swish apartments.

The Mermaid Theatre in London was revolutionary at the time: theatre in the round, theatre workshop. We used it as a launch-pad for a new range of fashion garments, and this was the first time a theatre had been used for such a thing, with music. It was an event, and made the headlines.

We went to see *Alfie* at the Mermaid Theatre, with an elderly female friend. The opening scene was a pair of knickers flying over a screen. There was an abortion scene, and the language was really confrontational. It was pretty full frontal. I asked our friend afterwards what she thought of it, and she said, 'Charming my dear, charming.' So tactful!

We went to a lot of lunchtime theatre; there were lunchtime movies at the Mermaid. There was a great artistic buzz going on. The Roundhouse put on really strange productions. One minute it would be Nicol Williamson playing demented Shakespeare; next it would be a mad French group swinging from the rafters spraying the audience with dubious liquid. There was an alarming trend in favour of hauling people out of the audience and pouring water on them or abusing them or mocking them in some way, or even taking their clothes off. 'Audience participation' happened everywhere, even in *Hair*, where you could dance on stage.

There was that feeling that we were at the cutting edge all across the cultural palette, which certainly hasn't been felt in Britain since. I'm not saying it was Berlin in the thirties, but

TONY ELLIOTT

Tony Elliott founded the listings magazine Time Out *in 1968, when he was 21.*

"I was away at school at Stowe until I escaped to London to live at home with my parents in Kensington and do my A-levels at Westminster College in 1965. It was magical because I fell in with a gang of slightly older students, bohemians rather than hippies, who knew about jazz and art movies. We'd go to see Manfred Mann at the Marquee, and the Pretty Things out at Wood Green. There was lots of fresh, New Wave contemporary culture going on – the stuff Jim Haynes was doing at the Arts Lab, Yoko Ono and her bottoms film, the Roundhouse and Underground films – that wasn't really covered in the London papers or in the desperately unhip *What's On* magazine. There was a bit in the *International Times,* but it wasn't very good. While I was at Keele University I went to the *IT* office and offered to do their listings for them, but they said no. I think I was just too young for them, and probably a bit more organized than they were. I never signed up for all that flowers and bells stuff, I was far too self-conscious even in my first hipster trousers from Carnaby Street. But in 1968 my aunt gave me £75 and I started *Time Out* – printed on a single fold-out sheet, the equivalent of eight pages. And it took off."

...DAYS I'LL REMEMBER...

there was a touch of that about it. Of happenings, happening everywhere. You could be in Harrods, or standing on Victoria Station, and suddenly a whole lot of people would start shouting or screaming or ringing bells.

There was a wonderful place called the Liquid Theatre, underneath the arches at Charing Cross, which was an excuse for a group grope. You went into a labyrinth; it was a bit dark and you were blindfolded, I think, and from the second you got in there you were touched and stroked, had interesting things fed to you, and drinks, and you lay in heaps with girls and men, you weren't quite sure, who writhed on you. This blissful procedure took about half an hour, with music and bells and incense, and when you opened your eyes again you were there with all these people, some of whom were, like you, customers, and some were part of the staff. It was all very innocent but fantastically sexy and liberating, and you knew that anybody over the age of thirty would disapprove.

Magazines and comix

1960 was the year *Mad* magazine came out in England. I remember a schoolfriend of mine's mother was a prominent actress and she'd been sent a preview copy. There was great excitement that this kind of wacky American humour, very new and very fresh, was suddenly available.

No 10 OZ **2/6**

new
easy
to
read
for
over
thirties

THE PORNOGRAPHY OF VIOLENCE

RICHARD NEVILLE

Richard Neville was one of the founders and editors of Oz *magazine.*

"On sexuality, it was important in the sixties to shake out old ideas and experiment with the new and find out how fundamental things like jealousy really are. Very fundamental, as it turned out. The notion that the world would be transformed by a group grope is whacko now, but remember, the Pill seemed benign, VD was under control and AIDS hadn't been invented yet. Our stand on drugs was tame; hard bad, soft okay. I never said shoot up and have a ball. A lot of good ideas came out of the upheaval, like the end of censorship and the missionary position, the rise of ethnic tolerance, playful collaboration, ecology. We may yet be proved right about the perils of rampant consumerism."

...DAYS I'LL REMEMBER...

I was a reader of comics until very late, but I graduated in the sixties to the *New Musical Express*. Once you did that, you couldn't read the *Melody Maker*. I read every word of it when it came out on Friday, including the footnotes on the back page. I'd memorize them.

Teen magazines only began with *Honey* in 1961, and I bought it religiously from the first issue, progressing from *Girl* and *Schoolfriend*. I can remember individual issues from 1964 and 1965 because each page was devoured so carefully.

There was a wonderful women's magazine called *Nova*, I was so sad when it folded. Before that, there'd been *Honey* and *19*. The focus was on fashion, and pop music, and boyfriends. They were so exciting, and very important—more so than books, at the time.

Private Eye was compulsory reading. I remember the Christmas issues with a little plastic record, always very funny.

We had two of the great chroniclers of the sixties in Maureen Cleave and Ray Connolly writing for the *Evening Standard*.

Brushes with the world we all should have been a part of, but weren't, were one of the highlights of the sixties. Magazines made you believe this; you took your cues from them.

The *Time* cover depicting Swinging London is a defining moment of the sixties. It was also the moment we *knew* we were in the middle of something big.

Muggeridge: is he Britain's biggest bore?
ane Fonda: men I'd like to have babies by if...
Veruschka: who's zoo in modelling!

We used to call each other names after characters in the underground comics. Bobo Bolinsky – 'He's the Number One Zero. He's No Big Deal' – was a popular choice, as were the Fabulous Furry Freak Brothers, especially Fat Freddie and his cat.

RAY CONNOLLY

Ray Connolly came to London from Liverpool in the early 1960s. After graduating from the LSE he became a reporter, and later branched out to write novels and screenplays. His first film was That'll Be the Day.

"One Saturday morning in May 1963, at the height of the Profumo rumour chase, I went across to Carnaby Street, which I'd just discovered, to buy a pair of hipster trousers. It wasn't a trendy or an ugly heritaged place then, just a cottage industry in a back street made up of half a dozen little shops, but the whole place seemed to be bubbling with a kind of my-generation energy I'd never come across before.

I was with some fellow students from the LSE who were, naturally, talking endlessly about Profumo, but all I could think that morning was that everything Profumo represented appeared to belong to a different world, which had nothing to do with me, other than to amuse me.

There he was, a middle-aged politician living a sad fifties lifestyle of crumbling privilege, trapped by his own deceit, doomed by his doxy and her pal, the blonde in the little petalled hat. And meanwhile a new generation – mine – was, like a guerrilla army high on optimism, humour, satire, impudence, style and music, already scaling the ramparts and breaking into the grounds of the Establishment. It was the very cusp of change, the moment when the torch of influence was being passed."

...DAYS I'LL REMEMBER...

The Sunday colour magazines came in in the sixties, about 1964 I think. They were the first lifestyle magazines, with good journalism and photography. Photography was a key art form of the sixties. Those pictures of the Rolling Stones rolling about, Marianne Faithfull lying on her tiger rug, couldn't have come from Pathé News or television. They also showed you what you could be eating, how you could be decorating your house, where you could be travelling. They had a real knack of picking on trends, or even inventing trends, and then pushing them like hell, so that for a while we really were setting the pace for everybody, including America. It was something you measured your status by. Keeping up with the Joneses suddenly became keeping up with the Jaggers.

Books

I remember reading *The Group* by Mary McCarthy when I was about fifteen, and then a notice going out from the headmistress that people were reading 'unsuitable literature'. A lot of that went on – a lot of censorship of literature by schools and colleges.

I went through a Hemingway phase in the sixties. Then I got into Russian authors; I became aware of foreign authors. But I also discovered British women writers: Iris Murdoch, Margaret Drabble. Andrea Newman, who used to write short stories for *Honey*.

We all read Edna O'Brien's *The Girl with Green Eyes* and *Girls in their Married Bliss*. 'The book can be read,' Edna O'Brien said, 'as a cold early morning signal to young girls – don't rush into marriage.'

My tutor at school asked me and my friend Gareth to tea one Sunday to meet some 'interesting friends' of his. Gareth and I got to his house that day to discover that W.H. Auden and Christopher Isherwood were the other guests. It was still, then, the era when being a schoolmaster was an honourable, venerable profession: you were a distinguished man of letters, essentially.

In those hedonistic days, if you had a telephonist/receptionist they didn't have to do anything else except answer the phone and look like a dolly bird. So I read copiously. I soon got off *Passionflowers in Honolulu* or whatever, and went up to Barker's book department and saw all these books with grey covers, the Penguin classics. So I though I'd have a go at those, and the first one I picked out was *Howard's End*. And I thought this is amazing, it was just wonderful. I went through all the Penguin classics without thinking they were hard, because they weren't. They were great stories, wonderfully written.

You had to be different then, so I started to read all these French novels by people like Zola and Balzac. Although I enjoyed them, I couldn't really talk about them because no one else had read them.

The first time I really got into reading was when Pepsi Cola had a free offer. If you collected three labels off the bottles and sent them in, you got a James Bond novel. I managed to get all the James Bond novels, and we read them and read them and loved them.

My reading was very trendy during my last year of school; I read most of Balzac's novels, Chateaubriand, Flaubert, Hemingway. But I didn't get around to James Joyce. In the summer of 1965 I took the Cambridge Scholarship English paper. We'd been warned that they sometimes threw in a trick question. The whole paper was writing an

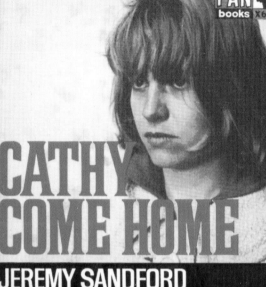

But when I finally read them they were amazing, just wonderful – at any rate, the first two books. It was the same with *The Lord of the Rings*, which I'd never read as a child. Those books alone justify the hippie philosophy.

I remember when I was in the sixth form in 1963 or so, and our English master asked if any of us had read *Catch 22*. I put my hand up, because we had it at home and I'd dipped into it, although I hadn't really understood it all that well. And I was the only one to put my hand up. So of course he asked me which bit I'd liked best, and I had to say the hospital scenes because they were the only ones I'd read. But when I did finally read it in 1966, I discovered that in fact the hospital scenes were some of the best in the book. Phew.

essay on a passage from literature. And I read the passage and thought, this is it, this is the trick question. So I wrote, basically, 'What a load of old cobblers!' And as we came out of the exam room my friend said to me, 'So, did you spot that it was a passage from *Ulysses*?'

The books *Billy Liar* and *The Loneliness of the Long-Distance Runner*, which I read when I was fifteen or sixteen, spoke louder to me than anything else.

I was interested in Kerouac and Ginsberg, although, like many a great mind of my generation, I never finished one of the books, just read a few pages to say I'd done so.

It took me a while to get around to reading the *Gormenghast* trilogy, in part because I was put off by its cult status among the more embarrassing of the ardent hippies.

Schooldaze

Secondary schools in the early sixties were still divided into public, grammar schools and secondary moderns. Children who failed the 11-plus had another chance when they took the 13-plus, but then that was it. Lots of people left school at 15: girls to serve in shops or as waitresses, or to become hairdressers; boys to take apprenticeships. Schools were run very much along the lines of our parents' days, and were pretty authoritarian and strict. But the winds of change were blowing. By mid-decade there was much more camaraderie between teachers and pupils, especially in the sixth form, and rules on school uniforms and hairstyles were being relaxed. There was a fairly traumatic time in between, however, when heads tried desperately – and vainly – to stem the tide of long hair for boys and mini skirts for girls.

'...a hand-grenade of a film... makes you laugh even as your blood chills... superb.'
EVENING NEWS

if....

daughters of gentlemen, and a lot of the girls went on to be debutantes and married chinless wonders.

I grew up in Liverpool and went to boarding school in Shropshire. We wore boaters, but it was just the local school, the kids came from the Midlands and Liverpool, shopkeepers' sons. It was probably the end of the era when ordinary people could send their children to boarding schools.

In 1960, as a thirteen-year-old schoolboy, my uniform was a pink blazer with dark grey trimmings, a pink cap, and short grey trousers.

I was sent to boarding school in 1961 and we were supposed to wear short trousers and short-sleeved shirts all year round. The uniform included six stiff white collars for shirts for Sunday wear. I never ever wore them, because that change happened just as I got there: that shift whereby traditions no longer held sway. When I arrived you had to have a cold bath every morning. The junior house was a kind of Nissen hut, and the prefects would stand in the bathroom and make sure you put your shoulders under the water. But by the beginning of my second term this tradition had been abandoned.

At the beginning of 1960 I was at a girls' boarding school in Hertfordshire. The education we got was hopeless. We got a good smattering in English and History, and that was it, that was all girls were meant to know about, then. We learnt to make conversation, to knit and to sew. It was nineteenth-century education for the

I came from a village where more or less everyone went to the local church school from age five to fourteen then left. But my mother decided that I would go to a grammar school, so when the sixties began I found myself among this new lot of people, doing unheard-of things like learning Latin.

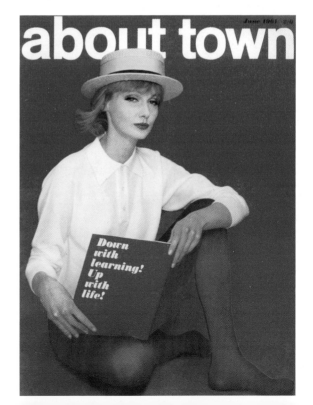

about town

June 1961

Down with learning! Up with life!

My O-level History notebook of 1961 was identical to my brother's history notebook, which he had done five years before, because the same teacher was dictating the same set of notes. It was rote learning. I never learnt to appreciate literature, I only learnt how to tick things off and pass exams. I don't remember ever *thinking* at all.

When I was twelve, I made the decision that I would go into the commercial stream at school rather than the academic. After a year, I realized that this was utterly wrong, so I asked if I could change. And I was told no, of course you can't.

I went to a girls' high school which had none of the clubs and societies that happen now. It was straight academic. Hockey, netball and tennis were the preoccupations; nothing social was encouraged. The only time we got together with the boys' high equivalent was for a play.

My school recently had a 30th reunion of our leaving, and during the evening we were all handed a copy of a letter from the headmaster to the parents dated 1 September 1965. To me, this letter sums up the first half of the sixties. It reads:

'Dear Parents,
In my opinion, there has been a decline over the past year in the attention members of the school give to their personal appearance. It started with this matter of hair. A few senior boys began adopting long, girlish hairstyles associated with some pop singers. This seemed harmless enough, and I expected them to grow out of it. But recently younger boys, falling under their spell, have copied them, and school as a whole has an increasingly unkempt look. Quite frankly, I am tired of seeing hair creeping over coat collars and over ears, down the face, and in a few extreme cases falling over the eyes, interfering with games and physical activity. With it goes a disregard for clothes and shoes, and at times a sullen look, taken, I imagine, from the popular image of what modern young

people should look like… If your son is one of the shaggy minority, or one of those likely to copy those who are, I ask that you send him back at the beginning of next term with his hair cut reasonably short, and, with your encouragement, to take more pride in his appearance.'

Isn't that marvellous? The sixties was that time; there was a dramatic change. The generation gap was more obvious than it ever had been before.

I remember the long school photograph, with everyone at the school in it. And there was always a person who was going to run from one end of it to the other, so they could appear twice.

When I wasn't doing so well at school, it was still an age when my father thought he could fix me up to get into Oxford or Cambridge, like he'd done with my brother, but those days had gone.

In 1966 or 67, we had a strike over school uniform, and everyone turned up in their Levi's. So everyone was sent home, and came back next day in their Levi's. Eventually, the rules were changed so that the sixth formers could wear Levi's as long as they wore the rest of the uniform, including the tie.

I got beaten a few times, with a slipper or a cane.

We did some amazing things at school. We started a film club, and people like Ralph Richardson came in, Lindsay Anderson and other famous people, and they'd donate something such as a camera to the club.

In my last year of school, in 1965, there was a real feeling of – rebellion isn't quite the word; there were a lot of changes happening in the school about the treatment of boys, especially in the sixth form; there was a lot of backing off from enforcing really strict rules about dress, hair, smoking.

I went to a co-ed school, but even so there was nothing like the companionship that my own children have had in their schools. There was no friendship between the sexes then; if you made contact with a boy, it was automatically considered to be sexual. If you talked to somebody, your friends would ask, 'Are you going out with him?'

I meant to keep my school hat as a souvenir, but on our very last day of school in 1965 all our hats were collected by two girls and strung up with lots of pairs of navy-blue knickers, and hung from the school chimney.

The wonderful thing about my school was that it taught me that I could be anything, do anything. We had lots of intellectual female role models, and lots of girls went on to do science, and so on. It was a pioneering girls' grammar school and it was wonderful.

A girl at school who was extremely well endowed was nicknamed 'Stacks'. She also happened to be brilliant at maths, and we were all astonished at this. Girls as well as boys, we were amazed that a curvy girl could be a maths genius.

I did A-level Economic History, and I was the only girl in a class of twenty or so. I beat the pants off all of them in the mock A-level exam in 1965, and that caused major resentment. *Major* resentment.

At assembly each morning, we older girls were at the back on the side nearest the exit, and when assembly was finished we had to file out the whole length of the hall under the scrutiny of all the boys on the side opposite the exit. It was hideous; like running the gauntlet every single morning, feeling all those male eyes on you, sizing you up.

School was of course part of my everyday life but it didn't feel important at the time. Things that went on outside school were much more important: youth club, lads and dances. All the things that made you stop and think and challenge what was going on – things like *That Was The Week That Was* – happened outside of school.

I took my A-levels a year early, then spent a year doing nothing much. Nowadays you'd have a gap year, go off and do something exciting, but as it was I just hung on at school doing nothing, wasting my time. It was pathetic. And nobody suggested that I did anything else.

Boppin' at the high school hop

We used to have senior school dances, they'd bus in the girls from boarding schools around Wiltshire and Dorset. A master and mistress would always have to start the dancing off,

VIVE AUDACTER

because all the girls were at one side of the room and all we boys at the other. A three-piece band would be hired from Bournemouth: a clarinet, someone on piano, and a drummer who sat there swishing away monotonously. They wore dinner jackets with shiny pants, and they'd play things like 'Desafinado', 'Tea for Two', and they were totally uninterested in the whole thing.

There was always a Paul Jones, and the idea was to end up with someone who looked reasonable. At my first school dance, I ended up with a girl with braces on her teeth and I took her outside and backed her into a holly bush. I met her again years later and she batted for the other side – maybe because of me.

We used to do the conventional, bog standard Christmas party at school. All games were cancelled for the month before, and you had to rehearse the Gay Gordons and the Valeta and the Military Two-Step. The best one was the one where you could

kick the person in front of you in the bum. Everybody did it, so you were flinching while you were doing it.

Extra-curricular activities

The 'school trip' was the only thing that mattered. We went over to Germany, Austria and Italy thinking that we were the best. We won the war, God was in his heaven and we were at the top of the pecking order. Big mistake. Their standard of living was so much better than ours and I realised what a con we'd all been fed by the Establishment. Everything was so much more colourful. It had a big effect on the way I viewed Britain from then on. I think that the exposure to foreign ways was one of several reasons for so much change in Britain in the sixties. It was the first time that the working classes had gone abroad without having to kill someone.

The big thing at school, apart from getting cars and taking an interest in girls, was drinking. As fifth formers, we used to go up to our local pub at lunchtime and play darts and drink beer. In those days the toilets were always outside, so one day I went out to take a leak and there were all these planks and tins and things in the way. I climbed over them, went in, and as I was standing there having a pee all the cement that formed the urinal began to disintegrate, falling and crumbling in a great big heap. I thought, bloody hell, this beer's strong, then shortly afterwards the builder came in and berated me because he was renovating and the new cement hadn't set yet.

We used to go to the pub at lunchtime, and we were too young to be served beer, but the landlord would serve us cider in the jug and bottle place, a cubicle where you could get cider as a thirteen- or fourteen-year-old.

Drinking was a huge thing at school, mainly because it was hard to get out and about at night – none of us had cars, and public transport was pathetic – so our social life revolved around drinking at lunchtime. I got a fair bit of practice in at being drunk before I went to university. The teachers would drink at lunchtime, too. Not in the same pub; we kept to separate establishments.

Beer was about 2/- a pint, and we'd get 1/6d dinner money so we'd get six of chips or three of chips and a bread roll, then you could go and get half a pint – in your school blazer. We'd go drinking at night, too, when I was fourteen, and not a very tall fourteen either. Landlords didn't seem too fussed in those days; they wanted the dough. They did stick us in the back bar, though.

Youth clubs, coffee bars and cigarettes

In the early sixties I belonged, not for religious reasons but for social reasons, to a Baptist Church Fellowship. They had socials which were totally innocuous; lemonade and cheese and biscuits.

My life revolved around the church and its social activities. It provided the youth club, friends, trips; it was a major part of my life.

It would be really unfair to be condescending about the church youth club I went to. At the time, it was great: dancing, music, records, snooker, darts, trips out, socials. At the socials we'd play games like Postman's Knock and Winking. In Winking, all the lads would stand behind a circle of chairs, and there'd be one empty chair. The person who had the empty chair could wink at any girl who was sitting on a chair in the circle, and she'd have to come and sit on his chair and give him a kiss. Winking was a great game.

The Methodist Youth Club was really important to us in the early sixties. It was terribly innocent but we had fabulous times there, just sitting about nattering or playing badminton, cards, or table tennis. We weren't interested in religion at all. Going home from the youth club was wonderful, too, because you could walk home with lads. You'd call at the chippie on the way.

In 1963 in Burton, when we should have been studying for O-levels, we began to go down to the Kavern Koffee Bar, near the bus station. It was underground and as nasty as could be. It was the nearest we could get to the real thing. Dark, hidden and dismal. It was also important that we should not have been going there.

Even in Abingdon, Oxfordshire, there was a frothy coffee café called the Mousehole, underneath the Town Hall. We would cycle in from school through the cold winter winds and sit there drinking frothy coffee and looking with indescribable envy at the Teddy boys and girls who played the juke box.

The Bis Bar in Sunderland was the first coffee bar we went to. You had to go there on a Saturday morning; anybody who was anybody went there, wearing a sheepskin jacket.

Once we started to go to coffee bars we all started to smoke. We didn't have a library at school so we were allowed out, and we'd go straight to a coffee bar and start smoking.

When I came back from a holiday in Bulgaria in 1964 I was smoking those tiny different-coloured cigarettes called Sobranie Cocktail, I think; smelly things, but I felt so cool. Gitanes were also considered really cool.

After *Breakfast at Tiffany's* there was a great vogue for very long cigarette holders. So I got one, and I'd sit there with this huge thing, in danger of lighting up other people's hair, thinking, I do look like Audrey Hepburn, I do, I do, and of course I didn't.

THE JAY TWINS

The Jay Twins, Helen and Catherine, were famous for being the long-legged blonde twin daughters of the Cabinet Minister Douglas Jay, for going to the new Sussex University (they made it the most popular university choice in 1966–7) and for wearing their Courrèges boots to a Buckingham Palace garden party.

"It all started when Max Hastings interviewed us for the *'Londoner's Diary'* of the *Evening Standard* wearing our long boots from Anello & Davide. For a few years in the mid-sixties we couldn't even get on our bikes without being photographed, and written about in *Honey* and *Tatler*. Fame isn't really a good idea unless it's based on some talent, which ours wasn't – the IT girl syndrome. We weren't even dress designers, we just had the right figures and faces and our father was a government minister. At Sussex we were always being pursued by paparazzi or whisked away to some television studio to give 'the teenage angle', but the university authorities never stepped in to say it had to stop. And we were pre-drugs. We all had such a good time we didn't need drugs. I suppose we were what is now called 'famous for 15 minutes'. But it was tremendous fun and we didn't take it too seriously."

...DAYS I'LL REMEMBER...

I rolled liquorice-paper Old Holborn cigarettes for a long time; I thought that was cool. We were constantly trying to pretend that we were less respectable than we were, I think.

Virtually everyone smoked then. You not only had to remember whose round it was for drinks, you had to remember whose round it was for fags. If anyone didn't buy a round or pass out the cigarettes, we thought it was outrageous.

College days

1965 neatly divides the sixties, and it changed my life totally. Before then it was church youth club, school, sport and pop music; in 1965 I went to university. Part of the change in my life was stopping all conventions when I left home, so for the first term I didn't wash or cut my hair once.

I was filthy. I didn't go to many lectures. All standards of civilized existence disappeared. Then I got home at Christmas and realized I was being ridiculous.

It was only when I went to college in 1963 that I felt I'd joined the teen-age, because before then I'd been a schoolgirl, and therefore restricted. You fantasized about freedom, and what you might be doing: listening to pop music, and going into smoky dives, and smoking. I didn't do any of that. So I was watching what was happening in the sixties from the sidelines, waiting to join in.

I didn't know anyone whose parents had been to college or university, and none of my friends did either. Yet we saw it as our right, even though we were the first generation who had such education available to us.

There was an inevitability about it all: you took your O-levels then your A-levels, then you went to university. And in fact no one from our background had ever gone to university before. But it didn't feel like a privilege or anything unusual at the time.

As a girl, going to college was all bound up with the whole Women's Lib thing. It seemed the most natural thing in the world, to go to university and compete with boys on an equal footing, yet that equality was in its infancy, really.

I had been placed in a girls' hall of residence. You were only allowed home twice a term, and you had to be in by half past ten every night unless you asked for a late pass. And yet we were right next door to a newly built co-ed 'student village' where people had total freedom. I had had more freedom at home than I had in college.

At ten o'clock every Saturday morning you had to go up to the dining hall in my hall of residence to collect your supplies for the weekend. These usually consisted of two eggs, a tin of curried beans, three slices of bread and an apple. Stupid stuff. I was horrified to discover that you were not allowed to cook onions because they made a smell. It was part of the written rules. You weren't allowed to wear rollers in public parts of the building, either.

During the week, dinner was always formal. There were long refectory tables, and a stage with high table. Every evening, certain students were invited to be guests at high table with the Warden and the moral tutors. Before that, you went into the Senior Common Room and had a glass of sherry. This was the most awful thing I could have ever imagined. I hadn't gone to university to be part of this charade, I thought. The people you had to talk to had nothing in common with ordinary people, they lived in a different world.

JULIAN BARNES

Julian Barnes, the novelist, was still up at Oxford in the summer of love.

"The sixties didn't happen until the seventies for most people – including me. I was at Oxford from 1964 to 1968, but there were so many different circles, and flower power affected only a very small number. I didn't know anyone who went on the Grosvenor Square march. I wore my hair long, and had a pair of purple jeans which were excruciatingly uncomfortable at the crotch; but I knew only one person who ever mentioned drugs. He would refer knowingly to 'big H and little h', which years later I presumed had meant heroin and hash; but this seemed a personal eccentricity rather than an interesting fashion. I knew about LSD because I'd read my Aldous Huxley, and about opium because of Cocteau and Francoise Sagan. Anyway, sex seemed such a hallucinatory business that you didn't seem to need any further additive. Apart from that, I suppose I kept my head down, working. I suppose I was sixties-ish in not thinking in any practical terms about the future, just blithely assuming things would turn out in some pleasant but undefined way."

...DAYS I'LL REMEMBER...

In that first month at university I met everyone who is still my friend. Apart from relatives, there is no one from the first eighteen years of my life that I have anything to do with.

I didn't want to go into a hall of residence at university, so I chose digs, where you live with a family. I arrived there in October 1966 wearing my best suit, carrying my suitcase, and knocked on the door expecting a loving family to welcome me. This harridan answered and acted like some nightmare landlady. She was only in it for the money, didn't care about *me* at all, or the other seven students she had living there.

The course I was doing at Chelsea College in 1967 was terrible, but living in London as a student was wonderful: Portobello Road, pubs and clubs, buying *Private Eye*. It was a new, exciting culture.

We seemed to spend the entire three years at university either sitting in the Student Union coffee bar, shredding polystyrene cups, listening to the Spencer Davis Group and generally 'festering', as we called it, or in the Union bar, playing table football and getting drunk.

The three years of my undergraduate life – 1965 to 1968 – I still regard as the Golden Age of my life. I've had better times since as regards personal success and family life, but those three years made me what I am.

Shared houses and other domestic horrors

About a million of us shared an enormous, perishing cold old house off Palatine Road in Manchester. The water in the washbasins would freeze over regularly, so we'd all have to wash in the Student Union. We had so many parties it's a wonder the neighbours survived. After one party the living room burnt down, something to do with the wiring and the record player being left on. I lost my copy of *Sergeant Pepper* in that fire. Still rankles.

The blokes in our house didn't have a clue how to look after themselves. I mean, I didn't have much clue, but I sort of knew the basics. One guy wanted to fry an egg for breakfast one morning but couldn't find any oil or fat. So he tried to use vinegar.

With four blokes sharing a flat we had a roster for cooking, but one bloke had no idea. He put a pan of chips on one night, then after about half an hour he came into the living room and complained that the chips weren't going brown. We asked if the fat had been hot enough when he put the chips into it. 'What fat?' We went out to the kitchen and found he'd been trying to cook them in water.

People were very cavalier with other people's property, as I recollect, especially with food and records and books. I still miss my copy of Ferlinghetti's *A Coney Island of the Mind* that was taken in 1969. But some people went to absurd lengths to protect their territory, writing their names on eggs and so on.

In 1966 I shared a bedsit in Hampstead with an old schoolfriend. It had two gas meters, one in the kitchen which took shillings, and one in the bathroom which took pennies. It cost 4d to have a bath. On Saturdays we'd put money on horses, cross our fingers and hope that we'd win so we could have a good weekend. We got up early to get the milk off other people's doorsteps.

A lot of my sixties memories are really grubby. I was desperately poor. I lived for a while in a tenement in Dundee, which was grotty, dark, damp and dirty. We shared a toilet with six other tenements, and we didn't have a bathroom in the building.

Food

Our attitudes to food were pretty primitive in the early sixties. In fact, mine remained that way for most of the decade. I started by being horribly sick when taken to Spain by my parents in 1962, because I couldn't stand the taste or even the smell of garlic. I kept the momentum when I first saw my sister cooking real spaghetti in 1964: I was astonished when I saw her feeding these long, stiff strands of pasta into a pan of boiling water, because I'd only ever seen or tasted tinned spaghetti before that.

I was worse than useless about food when I left home in 1965. I had never even eaten a tomato. I got through the sixties without eating anything different from the fifties at all. I can remember going to the Plaza, Manchester's first and best Indian restaurant, and ordering sausage and chips. They had to have that sort of thing on the menu, then. That was pretty much what we lived on in the sixties: beans on toast, fried eggs, chips, things like that.

In 1966 I bought Elizabeth David's Italian cooking book, because all you could get in restaurants – affordable ones, that is – was transport caff food.

People were just starting to go out to eat. I remember the Berni Inn in Worcester, where we'd go on Friday nights to have chicken in a basket and a glass of red wine, followed by an Irish coffee. Great fun.

We used to go to an Indian restaurant where you could get half a biriani for 2/6 – a plate of rice with almost pure chilli sauce and a couple of lumps of meat. People had drunk so much by the time they got there that all they could taste was chilli. It was the first Indian food I'd had.

The first time I was taken out to a meal in a pukka restaurant was to the Ark in Kensington. It was amazing, really classy. I had a Mont Blanc pudding; it was like a mountain, with chestnut puree in the middle, then round that it had pure whipped cream, then round that was meringue. It was all new and exciting.

Household style

I remember getting our first telephone when we moved down to London in 1960. In those days the exchanges had names as well as numbers; ours was ARNold 3062, because all the exchanges around us were named after poets.

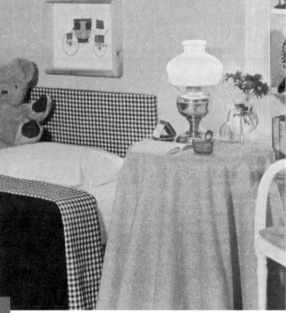

My Auntie Marjorie had her kitchen redone in the early sixties, mainly in orange. It even had orange spotty seats. I remember her telling us she thought it was really great, because 'it looks just like a snack bar'

Hardly any rental properties in the sixties had fridges. In summer you kept your milk in a pan of water on a shady windowsill.

I had a letterhead that read '84 St George's Square and so is the Pope'.

When I got to college in 1965 I couldn't phone home because my parents had no telephone, so they arranged to go to the local telephone box to call me at certain times each week.

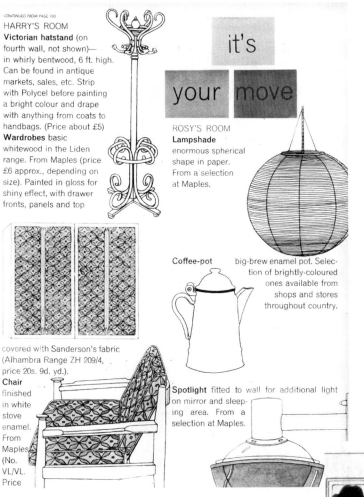

CONTINUED FROM PAGE 100

HARRY'S ROOM
Victorian hatstand (on fourth wall, not shown)—in whirly bentwood, 6 ft. high. Can be found in antique markets, sales, etc. Strip with Polycel before painting a bright colour and drape with anything from coats to handbags. (Price about £5)
Wardrobes basic whitewood in the Liden range. From Maples (price £6 approx., depending on size). Painted in gloss for shiny effect, with drawer fronts, panels and top

covered with Sanderson's fabric (Alhambra Range ZH 209/4, price 20s. 9d. yd.).
Chair finished in white stove enamel. From Maples (No. VL/VL. Price

it's your move

ROSY'S ROOM
Lampshade enormous spherical shape in paper. From a selection at Maples.

Coffee-pot big-brew enamel pot. Selection of brightly-coloured ones available from shops and stores throughout country.

Spotlight fitted to wall for additional light on mirror and sleeping area. From a selection at Maples.

The house had that décor that was a mix of classic eighteenth century Enlightenment and very pop, Baltic pine stuff. A great stash of vodka in the cellar, too. And we'd sit there and it felt that, vicariously, we were really in the thick of Swinging London.

All the new sixties furniture styles, Heals and Habitat and suchlike, were borrowed from Scandinavia. 'Isn't it good,' etc.

When I left home to go to university in 1966, I bought myself a portable record player for about £20 and a fake-fur, purple-backed cushion. I thought they were the height of chic. I bought myself a Joan Baez record, a Dylan and a Beatles, and I was all set.

We all had to have collages on our walls, pictures made of images torn or cut from magazines. I had one featuring the gorgeous model Veruschka, and lots of photos from *Honey*.

Friends moved down to London in the late sixties and got a flat in Holland Park. They painted all the walls dark purple, which I thought was so cool. You couldn't see a thing, but it was cool.

We only really became aware of interior décor at the end of the sixties, because until then it had been either fifties-style parental homes or student grot. Then everything had to be purple or black, or midnight blue.

In 1966 some friends of mine were house-sitting Peter and Wendy Cook's house in Church Row in Hampstead. They had a life-size model of Spotty Muldoon in the bedroom; you could press the stomach and it had a tape recorder inside going 'Hello, I'm Spotty Muldoon' in that famous voice.

Behaving badly

Of course we behaved badly. In the fifties, when teenagers were invented, they turned into Teddy boys and were really threatening. Mods and Rockers were renowned for bank holiday, seaside battles. We were less violent, but just as likely to get stuck into the booze. And we had something entirely new, to which some of us took with a vengeance: recreational drugs.

Booze

The first getting drunk was when I was about fourteen. I'd gone round to my friend's on my bike, and she'd got some bottles of Babycham. I must have had two bottles, and I couldn't get back on to my bike to ride home. I thought, 'Ooh, this is a really strange feeling.' I had to walk home.

We went to the local ballroom and a woman was on stage singing 'Climb Every Mountain'. We all joined in and I did my usual drunken thing of singing 20 octaves higher than everyone else. For some reason we went back the following night, and there was a request for members of the audience not to sing along with the act.

I had four older sisters, who had bottle parties in the early sixties – a hangover from the fifties. They lived on the top floor of our house, and their friends would come and bring a bottle and hand it to the barman, which was me, even though I was barely into my teens. So I discovered my love of alcohol early.

I first got drunk in 1964, when I was seventeen. Friends of my parents held a goldfish warming party, and they just kept filling my champagne glass. I ended up with the whirling pits, being sick in the bathroom for hours. It should have put me off booze forever, but alas it didn't.

We went up to London for the weekend during my first term at university and went straight out on the piss. I got legless, and fell over and gashed my head on the way back to the hotel. Blood everywhere. In the hotel room I collapsed on the floor and

. . . and no wine ever had a lovelier birthplace

The Palace of Mateus, Douro, Northern Portugal

Photograph by Percy Hennell

MATEUS ROSÉ

the enchanting pink wine

passed out. When I woke up I couldn't move. I panicked and thought I was paralysed, until I realized that my face was stuck firmly to the carpet with congealed blood.

When I was about fifteen I went to a really posh Chinese restaurant with my best friend and his family. Mr Hong's, I think it was, in London. I'd never eaten this type of food before, and, coupled with the red wine, it was too much for me. They dimmed the lights in the restaurant to sing 'Happy Birthday to You' to my friend and I fell arse over tit off my seat and slid underneath the next table, which was occupied by Lulu and one of the Gibb brothers (the Bee Gees).

Pubs were such a social scene. My father took me to my local, the Nag's Head, for the first time, when I was about seventeen. I certainly wasn't eighteen.

My father used to try to stuff us with gin and pastis. He thought that at any age you should be able to hold your liquor like a man, so we had to start early. He's now in his nineties and going strong.

I started going to staircase parties – parties held on staircases in the halls of residence at university – where you took a bottle of cheap cider or wine as your entrance ticket. They were terrific parties. They usually ended up with everyone being sick all over the stairs as they went out.

At sixteen I moved into a flat in Putney with a friend; you could do that, then. It was like moving to Hollywood or something. We did incredibly innocent, wild things, like get dressed up in long skirts, weird make-up and military jackets, and get drunk and have dinner in the flat, just the two of us. The corner shop sold bottles of wine for 7/4d, and it was absolutely awful stuff. We bought lots of it, and drank ourselves stupid.

ROBERT LACEY

Robert Lacey is the biographer of the Queen and Princess Grace and co-author of The Year 1000.

"I started off the sixties as a prefect wearing a school cap. Then I did Voluntary Service in Africa in long khaki shorts and knee-high socks. When I left university in 1967 the uniform was still cavalry twills and Hush Puppies. The caftans and beads that the Beatles wore were a sort of fancy dress you might put on if you went to a pop festival. As I remember it, the sixties didn't really permeate ordinary life until they were nearly over. But then I came to London, got myself a Beatles jacket, grew my hair – and never looked back."

...DAYS I'LL REMEMBER...

GENUINE
London Fog
CANNED IN LONDON

WHITBREAD
Pale Ale

Gentle Summer Rain
BOTTLED IN ENGLAND

Made for each other.

We had a huge party in our shared house, during which the toilet became completely blocked. It was a really revolting scene. The next morning we found one member of the household trying to clear the blockage with a saucepan.

A bunch of us students used to meet in a pub most weekends, and some of the regulars bitterly resented us. One particular old biddy would sit there shaking her fist at us and shouting, 'It's our taxes that pay for you louts!' I used to dream of coming across her on a zebra crossing and running her down. But in retrospect, she was right. She was paying for our grants, and our behaviour was pretty awful.

In our final year of university, in the late sixties, we developed the habit of pouring pints of beer over each other's heads. We thought it was great fun, but it got out of hand sometimes when the person the beer was being chucked at ducked and the innocent person at the next table copped the lot. Occasionally it got really out of hand, and there were fights, or threats of violence.

We went to the pub every single night. That's all we wanted to do: be adult enough to knock it back every night. We'd pour appalling stuff down our gullets, bull's blood. And Watney's Red Barrel was the only beer. Shocking stuff. All the good beer had disappeared, and the campaign for real ale hadn't started.

We'd have a bottle of gin between us all before we hit the nightclubs. If I had six gins I was sick, then I was all right.

Most of my bad behaviour was getting drunk. I seem to have been totally drunk for about fifteen years. I never saw certain people sober for years – including my future husband. We used to drink filthy stuff like giant bottles of Hirondelle wine and Party Sevens, and Number Four and London Pride sherry. You'd wake up in the morning not daring to open your eyes, wondering what it was going to be like.

I was always rather pleased it was all happening, but also always slightly tense, especially if we were doing something wrong. It was all wonderful, but I was never quite at ease when we were in pubs chanting obscenities or smashing glasses.

Most of the fights I saw in the sixties were really vicious, and over stupid things like someone spilling beer over someone's suede shoes. Glasses and bottles would be broken, and shoved into people's faces. It's much more civilized now, pubs are more civilized.

Those days seemed far safer. The word 'mugging' may have been in use in America, but it wasn't in England. In 1969 I lived in Moss Side in Manchester, and our landlord was West Indian. I used to go to a club with him after the pubs shut, and I'd be the only white guy there. I used to come out at two o'clock in the morning and walk home, and I never felt the slightest bit bothered or threatened.

We were drunk a lot – the obsession was with drinking ten pints every night. There was a men-only bar at the pub I went to in the mid-sixties; it was all sport and booze. There were no drugs at first. That was our salvation, perhaps. By the time drugs came along we'd got into the swing of drinking heavily, so when we got into dope we'd already had a skinful before starting to smoke. It kept you from being pretentious, which an awful lot of druggies could be.

Drugs

My boyfriend went up to Edinburgh University in 1964, and he rang me one night to tell me he was absolutely stoned out of his tree. I got terribly self-righteous and gave him a huge lecture about the dangers of drugs – and within a couple of years I was at university myself and hoeing merrily into whatever I could lay my hands on.

My brother-in-law was a minor drug dealer in the early sixties; one night he let me smoke some dope, even though I initially refused. He sat me down and told me all about marijuana. His advice to me was, don't take anything in a pill, just smoke dope. So I did.

One night at the J 'n' J Club – a fantastic dance club in Manchester where the sweat gathered on the ceiling and poured down like rain on the dancers – I noticed my boyfriend and a friend of his passing a cigarette between them. I told them there was no need to share as I had plenty of cigarettes – at which point, of course, it became clear that they were sharing what I then called a 'reefer'. I flew into a rage and lectured them all the way home. Eventually of course I tried it myself.

"*We have reason to believe you are carrying certain substances of a hallucinogenic nature.*"

asked me to roll a joint I couldn't have done. Except I was curious, and started smoking in the end.

I took some speed before going to a concert by Mountain at the Rainbow. Afterwards we went back to a friend's flat and smoked tincture. I had that 'If only my father could see me now!' feeling. All the middle class in me thinking, 'Ha ha ha, I'm with the druggies! I'm hitting the underground big time!' I wasn't at all, of course.

About ten of us – this was the real student life, wasn't it – would meet in a flat and put on very loud progressive rock music: Emerson, Lake and Palmer, Pink Floyd, Quintessence. Everybody would end up absolutely paralytic. I can remember being so stoned that I had to concentrate all my energies to get to the loo. And the drug squad coming to the flat and finding a packet of contraceptive pills in the dustbin.

I started taking drugs when I was about 14, in 1965, introduced to them by the older kids in my school. Money was very tight, sometimes I didn't get pocket money, but I scrounged and saved to scrape together 17/6d, and managed to buy some hashish. I spent the whole time laughing.

The first real drop-out I went out with was a guy who was part of the Liverpool 8 scene. We used to go back to people's 'pads'. I didn't know what to do, I didn't know how to go 'phew, phew, phew' – you know, inhaling deeply and noisily. If anyone had

Those early dope-smoking days were full of paranoia. We spent whole evenings twitching the curtains, convinced there were police surveillance cars parked opposite our house. And we made elaborate contingency plans for flushing the stash down the toilet in the event of a raid. Ha! I doubt the local constabulary gave us a moment's thought.

Getting stoned was fantastic in the beginning. I'd never felt such a thrill, sitting in darkened rooms with lots of other people, passing joints around and making sure I didn't bogart, listening to fabulous music by Family and Janis Joplin, Big Brother and the Holding Company, Pink Floyd, The Band, Cream, Yes, King Crimson, Love – oh, tons of wonderful stuff. And laughing, laughing so hard I thought I'd died and gone to heaven. I really miss smoking dope. I used to enjoy it enormously.

Dope was such a huge freedom thing, and a huge Us and Them barrier between us and our parents.

We used to 'score' in Moss Side. I'd drive and keep watch while the boys disappeared into dubious basement clubs, hoping they wouldn't be mugged or ripped off. We'd buy cherash, bush, Leb gold, Afghani or Paki black. Tiny amounts of hash, the size of a fingernail, for a quid or so. If it was your turn to roll the joint you had to be really careful when the block got down to the size of a pinhead. I can remember the shame and horror of being the one who lost the last piece. And frantic mornings spent combing through the hairy things you find down the backs of sofas or under the arms of chairs, trying to find the microscopic bit of hash lost the night before.

We didn't get on to acid until 1968 or so. It seemed really frightening at first; there were so many scare stories in the papers, and everyone seemed to know someone who knew someone who'd had a bad trip and ended up blind from staring at the sun, or in a loony bin. In the end we got really into it, but I always found the experience slightly disappointing, slightly contrived. You sat there and felt you ought to be experiencing all this enriching, tactile, sensuous stuff, and in reality you just felt slightly odd, jangly and jittery.

We had a wonderful time at the 'sit in' in 1969. Bands all night, lots of dope, a hall full of people grooving. I can't even remember what it was all about now, and I don't think it mattered that much at the time. The only downside was that it was freezing, and we all had to huddle together to keep warm. A couple of my friends rolled themselves in the floor mats that had been in front of the main doors – filthy mats, people had been tramping grey slush onto them all evening, but when you're stoned you don't care.

I'd never really believed the expression 'turning green' until a friend first tried dope. He didn't smoke cigarettes, but wanted to appear cool and accepted a joint one night. He turned the colour of pea soup.

For years, I didn't take any drugs. No one noticed, because it's really easy in a big group of people, nearly all stoned, just to pass on the joint without taking any yourself. But I bet my friends would have been astonished to know I didn't smoke.

The whole drug scene scared me. I think I thought, if I get into this at all, I'll get into it in a deep, deep way. And I don't like losing control. The people I knew in the drug scene were kind of scary people; criminal underground rather than alternative underground.

I had a very depressing, working-class background. But it kept my feet very firmly on the ground: I never did drugs. I used to watch people taking them; I was a great watcher and observer of what was going on. I used to watch this horrible greasy thing being passed around a group of people sitting on the floor and I'd think, ugh! Because if someone had put something in their mouth, you just didn't put it in yours. I couldn't bear the thought of someone else's spit in my mouth. I recently told someone that I never smoked dope and he said, 'But what did you do in the sixties?'

I only had one close friend who was a regular smoker of hash in those days, and he was always the object of scorn in the pub.

There was X, sitting staring vacantly in the corner of the cubicle in the union bar, and everyone would say, oh that's X, he's had a bad trip. That's all I knew about him. He never said anything. Was he a victim of the sixties? Would he have had just as bad an experience another time? We'll never know.

Even though I've never rolled a joint I thought smoking them was brilliant, because as soon as you had one you'd just sit around giggling. It was such a pleasant experience, and it seemed utterly harmless. But I did wonder if it made you lazy, because you drifted off into this nice dreamy world. Because I have this protestant ethic that anything that's enjoyable has to be suspicious, and you should spend most of your life working.

'I got you, babe': teenage romance

Until late in the decade the whole teenage romance thing was very much as it had been since time immemorial: girl meets boy, boy wants sex, girl either lets him (and loses him and/or ends up with baby) or doesn't let him (and loses him). Then along came the Pill, and a whole new world of carefree sex opened up. Except there was a price to pay eventually, of course. And mostly, women paid it.

The dating game

We were allowed a fair bit of leeway by our parents. We used to have these barbecues at a local caravan site, and wide boys from Swansea, who had Dansette record players, would come along. They had surf boards, and slicked-back hair, and they were like a different breed of animal.

My friend took me to a youth club and one of the older boys there – he was in the sixth form, while I was only fifteen – began to walk me home and we started kissing. I didn't like it at all; it seemed very wet and rather distasteful, and my mouth was all chewed to pieces.

I remember how unpleasant those early snogging sessions were, with saliva everywhere and teeth clashing and smelly breath and hideous sucking noises and a chin prickled to death by skin in need of a shave. You'd get a terrible rash later. It was all so different from what we'd been led to expect by fairytales and other romantic crap!

We used to go up a local tower and spit on the girls beneath from over the edge, like camels. The spit would go drifting down.

The worst moment of my life was finding out at school how children are conceived. Because I thought there's no way, ever, my parents could have done that! It was a real shock when I realized that there was no other way they could have done it. I was nearly sick.

When I was at school, boys were very much things to look at; creatures. We spied on them and talked about them, but we didn't interact. If you did, you were considered 'fast' and 'common'. Those girls always seemed to be having a good time, but of course they were common, and therefore despised. They had badly dyed hair, and were not expected to Get On in Life.

but there was something basically very sexy about them. They'd stand casually on the Waltzer taking your money – we'd be clinging on with both hands, and we'd think they were brilliant.

We started going to our friends' houses when their parents were out and playing Spin the Bottle and Postman's Knock. They were very innocent pursuits, but at the time they seemed like such naughty things to do.

Remember those warning lines about being frightened off when a boy starts breathing heavily, because that's when he can't stop? I used to read that in women's magazines, and imagine they'd start panting and go into some hysterical frenzy.

I was totally naïve about sexual relationships until I was about eighteen or nineteen. The first week at university, I met this girl and chatted her up – or rather, I thought I'd chatted her up, but she wandered off. The next morning I found her in my flatmate's bed.

In those days you had to wade through women's underwear. Normally, if you were lucky, it was a quick unsnap of the bra strap, panties down and you were right. But there were millions of configurations of bra straps. Every bra strap was different. You could spend half an hour trying to figure it out.

It was a nightmare wearing a pale-coloured jumper or blouse. You'd get home and just as you were walking in the front door you'd realize that the front of your jumper was covered in grubby fingermarks.

Virginity was our big problem. We still had it more or less intact in 1963. We wanted to keep it and lose it at the same time. We knew about sex, sort of knew what 'going all the way' meant. But there was a lot of mystique about virginity and we had grown up with all the talk about not losing it. It was drummed into us: Nice Girls Don't.

Our sole aim in life was meeting boys. That's what it was all about, really. Whatever you did, it was about where you could meet lads.

I thought the word 'crush' was invented for me: I was always desperately in love with someone, but it was never the person I was going out with. It was a real stigma not to have a girlfriend, so I always had one.

Funfairs were like a magnet. The rock music belting out, the Whip and the Big Dipper, the Big Wheel and the Wall of Death. They were an opportunity to meet rough lads. The minute they looked at us we were frightened to death, but it was exciting. They were greasy, horrible lads,

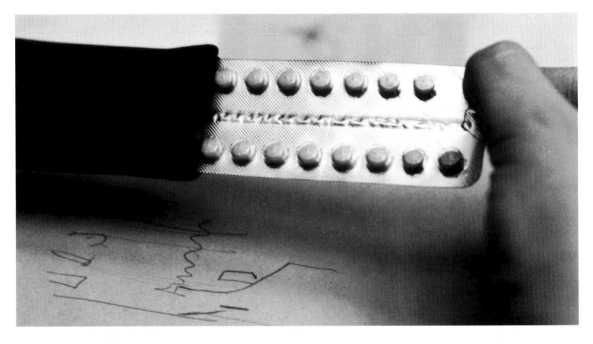

The local barber used to sell contraceptives. I was desperate to have sex, but I didn't know what to do. I couldn't buy them from him, in a small town – everybody would know. But I was terrified of getting girls pregnant, so I'd literally slept with several women before I actually had sex.

I remember going to school and saying 'Yeah, I've had sex!' to my male contemporaries—this was before any sex education was taught. I had no idea what was involved, and all I did was snog; heavy petting. The relationship lasted that one weekend, then that was that. It was mostly just misery, thinking about it and discussing it with friends. I found it very difficult to work it all out, even when they did start sex education classes.

I had a lot of failed affairs because I wasn't at all self-confident, but when the dam burst it was phenomenal. Getting emotionally involved was not good form; you had to be detached. Once I learnt that, I was very successful. Once you got over the hurdle of knowing what to do, it was pretty easy for us guys in the sixties.

A lot of the time, sex was a thing that you just looked at. There was a tremendous amount of enthusiastic snogging, but quite a lot of the girls I went out with behaved just as they would have twenty years earlier and said no, that's far enough.

When my boyfriend found out that his flatmate at university was gay he went ballistic. Kicked him out, refused to speak to him ever again, the works. It was terrible – but those attitudes were widespread. It was a brave man or woman who came out of the closet in the Swinging Sixties.

I had never heard of a homosexual, had no idea what the word meant, until I was eighteen. Then when I saw some men with umbrellas in 1965, I thought, oh, they must be homosexual. I'd never seen a man with an umbrella before. It's almost unbearable to remember my level of naïvety.

The cultural and sexual misunderstandings in those days were rampant. I had a full affair with an Italian man when I was living in Paris in 1963, who I thought was madly in love with me because he said so. He'd been back to

England with me for Christmas to meet my family, then it was summer and he was going back to Italy to see his family. So I assumed he'd invite me. And he looked at me as though I was mad, and said he couldn't possibly introduce his family to a girl whose own parents had been divorced—and while he didn't exactly say so, 'and who has also lost her virginity' was clearly implied.

'Free love'

The Pill became available to the public in 1961, but even in the late sixties its use among unmarried girls and women was frowned upon at best, seen as criminal at worst. To live together as an unmarried couple was extremely difficult outside trendy parts of London, landlords and ladies having yet to come to terms with the sexual revolution. The old morality had broken down, but nothing had come along to take its place. And we had the distinct – and probably correct – impression that the older generation didn't like us. And they especially didn't like our sexual freedom.

My thoughts were that you shouldn't really have sex until you were married; pre-marital sex was wrong. I felt very strongly about that. Although the fear of getting pregnant must have been a factor, too. But the whole free love aspect of the sixties completely passed me by.

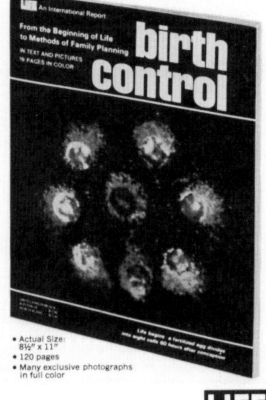

the lifestyle

My boyfriend and I wanted to live together at university in 1967, but in Manchester in those days it was absolutely impossible. It would also have been impossible to explain to our parents. So we used to rent two places then live in one – one of us sneaking in and out of the chosen flat in the hope that no other occupants realized there was a couple living there.

My sister went to see our local GP in London when she was seventeen, in 1963. She wanted a prescription for the Pill. Instead, she got a lecture followed by the shouted admonition: 'Wait until you are married!'

It was really difficult to get on the Pill even in 1967, the height of the 'free love' era. I was at Manchester University and there wasn't a doctor within miles who would prescribe the Pill to the students. Then word got around that an old, sympathetic doctor out at Eccles – miles away on the train – was giving out prescriptions. I trundled out there and was duly given the precious piece of paper. All of us who made the journey forever after called the Pill 'Eccles cakes'.

The worst moment about spending a night with a guy, in the early days, was waking up in the morning and knowing he'd see me without my eye make-up on. I knew he'd go off me then!

I cohabited with my boyfriend from 1966. I remember sitting my mother down and telling her that I was moving into a flat with Chris, but that we weren't going to get married, and expecting the balloon to go up. And she said, 'Oh well, you'll need some double bedding then, won't you?' and she took me out and bought me blankets and a set of sheets.

There was a lot of very casual sex for a number of years there. Looking back, I feel slightly embarrassed. On the other hand, do it while you can...

Unmarried mothers

Unmarried motherhood still carried a lingering stigma, although the winds of kinder change were stirring. But the norm was still to either have an abortion – if you had the nous and the wherewithal – or have the baby adopted.

Pregnancy was such a terrible, terrible thing to happen if you weren't married. It was talked about in whispers, and you reeled back in horror when you heard that so-and-so was pregnant. It happened to my cousin when she was sxteen, and it was the most awful thing for the whole family, a very significant event.

The girls who had babies while we were at school completely stuffed up their lives – their early lives, at any rate. You'd see them around town, dragging babies and pushing prams, looking about forty when they were nineteen. It was so sad.

None of us wanted to get pregnant. We wanted to be free. To live life. Then the magic drug came along just at the right time. But unmarried girls weren't allowed the Pill then. We just read about it in newspapers. Girls' magazines didn't write about contraception in those days. In March 1967, *Honey* ran their first feature on 'Birth control and the single girl'. I cut it out. Abortion didn't become legal until later that year.

People forget how conservative society at large was in the late sixties. In 1968, Dennis Tanner and Jenny Sutton of *Coronation Street* slept together before they got married, and there was such a stink in the papers.

I had an old Morris Minor, and several sexual episodes occurred in that. It was because you had nowhere else to go.

I had a baby in 1966, when I was unmarried. That era, to me, was one of increasing tolerance. My parents were very tolerant, and I stayed at home the whole time. I did have pressure from social workers to have the baby adopted, but when I put my foot down they said 'Oh, OK', and it was fine. I didn't feel an outcast at all. This was the first time single mothers were tolerated, accepted. I never, ever encountered any attitude. It was starting to be the thing to do, then: film stars, and people in the limelight, were having kids without marrying the fathers, so it became more accepted. In the fifties, it would have been disastrous. So I'm very fond of the sixties.

I had a gorgeous baby during my first year at university in 1965, she was absolutely lovely, but I didn't love her. I didn't find it at all traumatic to give her up for adoption. She'll be thirty-something now; she hasn't contacted me, and I haven't contacted her. I think I was too young and too selfish.

A well kept Secret . . . . . Smartly styled dress in pure wool with miniature checks. Crisp white detachable collar and patent trimming. Colours: Charcoal; Royal; Autumn Brown; Olive Green £5.5.0
Also Grey Flannel £6.6.0

MOTHERHOOD

25 BAKER STREET LONDON W.1

TELEPHONE WEL 4549

My friend Viv had a baby when she was seventeen, and we were all really amazed because we knew it had been conceived in a bubble car. I mean, how on earth do you manage to do it in a bubble car? But that was the only place they could go.

It was 1967, but before the Abortion Act, when I first became pregnant. I tramped around all the Harley Street doctors. I had to get a letter from a psychiatrist saying I was not fit to have a baby. That cost 10 guineas. Then the female doctor kept me sitting in the hall while she ate her dinner. She told me I was two and a half months, that she would book me in for the next week and that it would be 150 guineas – in cash.

I had an abortion in the late sixties, and I can remember sitting in a room in a Harley Street clinic where nobody else spoke English, but they were all clutching their cash. The girls were flooding across from Europe, because abortion hadn't been legalized anywhere else. You had to have two psychiatrists' reports, but they were all trumped up anyway.

As I left the abortion ward the doctor said, 'Take the Pill and don't come back.' I got back into the swing of life. There was no grief, nothing.

Wheels

For many of us, the sixties meant getting our own wheels for the first time. Scooters, motorbikes, cars… wheels meant mobility, wheels meant freedom. For James Bond wannabes, the E-type Jaguar was launched in 1960. But the ultimate wheels for ordinary young people – until Easy Rider made Harley Davidsons the Holy Grail in 1969 – was the Mini car, launched in 1962. Red was the preferred colour, of course. But we had little concept of socially acceptable driving…

Drunk driving just didn't seem to be a sin in the sixties. We all drank and drove. We drove while paralytic, at times. I remember once being a passenger in the back seat and thinking it a hilarious prank to put my hands over the eyes of the driver in the seat in front of me.

I borrowed my dad's Ford Anglia to go on holiday to Devon in 1967. On the motorway on the way there, we suddenly realized we were going the wrong way. So we just turned around, did a U-turn across the central reservation, and there was not a car coming in either direction, there was so little traffic in those days. In Devon we'd drink until we couldn't stand up, then we'd get in the car and try to drive back to the farm.

The days of old bangers went out with the MOT test, but in the sixties lots of people had cars that they'd bought for 50 quid. They weren't just mechanical wrecks, the bodywork had gone as well. Death traps. Doors had to be tied with string; floors had rusted through so you had to put metal plates over the hole or your feet would go through. Some grew fungus. And about 15 people would pile in. But there was hardly any traffic, so it was relatively safe to drive these cars around.

When mods grew out of scooters, they turned to motors. You had to have a Mini Cooper. You took the hub caps off and put wheel spacers on – which had the effect of making the whole thing structurally unsound, but that was neither here nor there. You had to have a straight-through exhaust pipe with no baffles, so it was really loud. And what you did on Saturday afternoons was, you belted up and down Guildford High Street, flat out in second gear, making as much noise as possible.

I had an Ariel Arrow motorbike, which was a 200 cc twin. Then I had a 500 cc Norton, with a state-of-the-art frame called a featherbed frame which was used on racing bikes. I even had one Japanese bike when

they first came out, a Yamaha. It was a bit like riding a sewing machine – they made the same sort of noise.

Minis were really spunky little cars, but they were essentially city cars. They weren't meant to be driven all over Europe. We drove one to Rome in 1964 and had so many breakdowns on the way. We had to sell it in Paris on the way back to get the fare home.

I got my first car in 1968, a Morris Minor that cost me £30. I drove it in triumph down to London to show my parents, but had to be rescued by my father about 20 miles from home when steam started pouring and hissing out of the bonnet. We left it at a garage and went to pick it up the next day. I'd had no idea you had to check the radiator and top up the water, so of course it had run dry.

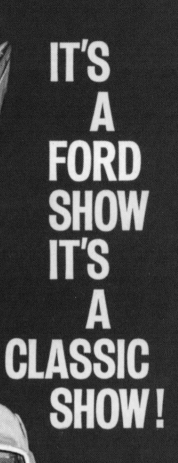

IT'S
A
FORD
SHOW
IT'S
A
CLASSIC
SHOW!

FORD
CAPRI
ZEPHYR
ANGLIA
CLASSIC

All the young men my friends and I knew had sports cars, mostly pretty cheap ones; it was the look that mattered, not the performance. Austin Healey Sprites were popular, and Triumph Heralds with no top. My friend Joanne had a Spitfire, and we'd drive around in that thinking we were the bee's knees, wearing sunglasses and headsquares.

The travel explosion

One of the innovations that differentiated the sixties from previous decades was the sudden availability of travel to the ordinary person. For the first time ever, families were able to holiday abroad; students of very little means headed off overseas; even travelling around Britain took on a new and exciting significance.

In 1964 I dragged my friend Marion off to hitchhike around France, so we could meet Sartre and become intellectuals. And we had nearly all our dreams fulfilled: we were arrested for sleeping rough under the bridges of Paris, and went around with this beatnik group. Oh God, it was everything I'd ever hoped for. It existed; it was out there. It was wonderful. Getting arrested was such a cachet, being herded into the police cell by these Parisian cops. And there were all these young people in France, sitting under the arches with their bell-bottomed jeans and long hair. It was like finding the Holy Grail.

Gaytours

sunshine holidays 1968

Gayflights from London Manchester & Newcastle

In 1965, two friends and I took a Mini all the way across Europe and down through Yugoslavia and into Greece. We spent seven shillings a day between us, and asked at the back of restaurants for their leftovers, that sort of thing; we were very proud of our Jack Kerouac approach to things, despite the Mini. Two of us had Beatle haircuts, and of course we had this Mini, which for many people overseas summed up that Swinging London thing. So there were parts of Greece, tiny villages and mountain towns, where the sight of the Mini would have the people pouring out into the streets. Then, when they saw that 'Beatles' were members of the crew of this little car, they went absolutely wild, and the most extraordinary generosity came our way. But at least three times a day we had to sing what we remembered of the Beatles repertoire.

I was a kitchen hand at Butlins at Barry Island in the three months between finishing school and going to university, in 1966. I had a brilliant time. There were lots of students from overseas there, and after my English upbringing, thinking we ruled the world, we were the best, it was a revelation. We'd been taught to hate the Germans, but I went to Germany after that stint at Butlins, to visit some people I'd met there, and I realized that they didn't hate us. They loved Bobby Charlton! It changed my life.

When we went to the South of France we used a tip given by Katie Boyle. She said, instead of using suntan cream, use olive oil mixed with vinegar. We were burnt to a crisp. Silly cow.

A group of us went on a camping trip to Turkey in the very first model Ford Cortina in 1964; an odd group, from Merseyside, South Wales, Lincolnshire. There were three of us from school, plus our music teacher and his girlfriend. We made a trip through places I'd barely heard of, like Romania, Bulgaria, Yugoslavia. It really opened my eyes to the fact that Britain was a tiny little place. We were astonished at the poverty.

In 1965 my boyfriend and I decided we'd go off and live in Greece for a while. We lived on Lindos, in a very arty community full of writers and photographers and poets and weavers. I felt a bit out of it, with my secretarial background, but I very much wanted to be in it.

During my first term at university in 1966 I went to Canada via BUNAC (British Universities North America Club) and promptly got pregnant via someone in Hamilton, Ontario, and had the baby adopted. There's a whole generation of adopted children out there.

We did a lot of hitchhiking. I remember hitching from Paris to Le Havre, and back from Southampton to Wales, regularly. It was quite normal then, but no one in their right mind would do it now, would they? Especially not girls or women.

The place to get adventure in 1967 and '68 was America, or at least abroad. Flower-power had hit America, but in English provincial towns such a romantic notion never really came to life.

I spent two summer seasons in Spain, in 1968–9. I drove down on my motorbike and worked in a bar in Fuengirola. I stayed nine months the second season, and it only rained for

one day the whole time. We rented a flat on Avenida de Mijas, starting with four of us, then, as we got greedy, it ended with about fifteen of us. But we weren't hippies: it was really difficult to be a hippie in Spain then. If anyone looked remotely scruffy they'd be kicked off the beach and hauled into gaol.

In the summer of '69 a group of us – five blokes and me – bought an old Commer van for £15 and set out for Spain. We only made it as far as Bordeaux before it conked out. Then I think we personally sank the AA's Five-Star insurance scheme, which we'd taken out before we left England for a couple of quid. The scheme paid for us to hire two cars to drive on down to Spain, where we stayed at a campsite for two weeks, living on bread and tomatoes and Cubalibres. Then it paid for all of us to get back to England by rail and ferry. The cherry on the pie was that it also paid to have the van towed back to England, where it arrived on our doorstep one day months later. It was a complete wreck, but there it was. We hadn't a clue what to do with it, so we ended up giving it to our landlord.

First jobs

I went to secretarial college in September 1960 for a year's course, which was very dreary. It covered not only shorthand and typing but also civics, office practice etc. They asked me what sort of work I'd like to do, and I said, well, I like reading. So they sent me to some publishing companies, and they all gave me interviews, and they all offered me jobs. Full employment, or virtually full employment, had a very big impact. I mean, to come out of some ordinary little secretarial college and just walk into a job in the area of your choice was what we took for granted. Magic!

I left school at sixteen in 1962. My mother arranged an interview for me with the local bank manager. I thought I'd work in the bank until I was eighteen, when I expected to go to teacher's training college. You only needed five O-levels to get in, then, and I had eight. But I ended up staying in the bank. I started work there at £350 a year, £6 a week, which was an amazing amount of money. I could do anything I wanted to on that amount, living at home. I never even considered leaving home, I didn't know about getting flats and things; it definitely wasn't an option.

I was always known as Miss Everett at work, and other people were called Mr So-and-So or Miss or Mrs So-and-So, even best friends. It's just the way it was.

In 1961 I earned 9 guineas a week, and I had a bedsitter in Hyde Park Gate that cost 3 guineas a week, which was precisely the recommended ratio.

In 1963 I decided I was going to live somewhere foreign, so I went over to Paris and got a job with the OECD at what seemed to me an extraordinary amount of money: I'd come from £9 a week, and they were offering me £20, tax-free, with a shop that sold tax-free grog and perfume, and a subsidized canteen where the food was fabulous.

LIBBY PURVES

Libby Purves, broadcaster and writer, was about to go up to Oxford in the late sixties. "I was a diplo-brat, and my parents were living in Hamburg, so in my gap year I worked for a German bank as a typist. This was a Bristow-like office where the men wore white nylon shirts and the women's skirts had to be over the knee and everyone was formally addressed—'Guten Morgen, Fraulein Purves'. Then I came over to London to visit my friend Fiona who was temping in Shepherd Market, Mayfair, and the culture shock was total. The ads in the tube said, 'Hey girls, like to work for two fun guys, Mikey and Dave?' It was like coming out of China. I watched Fiona's boss ask her to type something and she said, 'Piss off, baby.' And we'd walk down the King's Road in pelmet skirts and Courrèges boots and breathed the same air as Mary Quant. Everything in Britain seemed so laidback and unbuttoned, everyone just arsing around. So while Germany was creating an economic miracle, we slid majestically into our decline."

...DAYS I'LL REMEMBER...

When I left school at sixteen in 1964 I answered an ad in the *Evening Standard* for a receptionist/telephonist at an art publisher's in Kensington. They said, can you work a switchboard? and I said, yes (I'd never seen one before), and they employed me. The company was owned by chaps who'd been to Eton, the Guards, the City, then they decided that art would be a good thing to go into. It was all to do with that sixties thing of everything opening up. They'd always employed debs before, cousins of the Queen and so on. But they suddenly thought they'd get a prole, so they put an ad in the paper the very day I was looking. I was paid £6 a week. My weekly ticket to get from Raynes Park to Kensington cost something like 17/6, and I gave my mother 30 bob a week for my keep.

My first job after leaving school in 1965 was working as a stagehand at the Scala Theatre off Tottenham Court Road. The NATKE (National Association of Theatrical and Kine Employees, a powerful union now long gone) rate was 16/1d per performance; we got paid slightly under that, but there were phantom employees called Horatio Nelson and Napoleon Bonaparte, and you'd get someone to sign for them and you'd split their pay up between you.

My first paid full-time job, as opposed to Saturday work in shops, was as an unqualified temporary assistant teacher in 1966, between school and university. I worked in a girls' primary school in a fairly deprived part of London. The children were over 70 per cent immigrant, and many didn't know English. My first job was to take a group of them and try to teach them English. We had no classroom, so we sat on the stage in the school hall while P.E. lessons were going on around us. We mostly just sat and smiled at each other.

In 1966 I started a job in a merchant bank, which was the opposite of everything the sixties stood for. I was paid £1,000 a year as a clerk. I went to work every day in a white stiff collar with a stud, I had a very smart grey city overcoat and I was miserable. I had an adding machine at my desk, and I spent entire days counting either money or cheques or bills of lading. Just as the terrible constraints of workaday life in the city were clamping around me, I realized that this was the sixties, and if I wasn't careful it was going to be gone and I wouldn't have had much of it. The King's Road was there as a kind of terrific temptation; Carnaby Street was flourishing. So after 11 months of feeling miserable all week and freaking out at weekends, I resigned.

Behold the Bowler...

... austere, but sensitive. Why do I wear it? I wear it to acknowledge a human bank manager. My Westminster Bank manager. Two days ago (I'd gone to see him about that little windfall from my godfather) he eased the agony of explanation by arguing Puccini versus Wagner. (I'm opera mad.) Well, I mean, if someone can come that far to meet me, I can return the compliment. Hence the Bowler. You know, I think it rather suits me. Certainly the Westminster does.

Like to know more about us? Our booklet 'On using your bank' will answer your questions. Ask for a copy at any branch (the addresses are in the Telephone Book) or send a postcard to Public Relations Department, Westminster Bank Limited, 41 Lothbury, London E.C.2.

WESTMINSTER BANK IS FOR EVERYBODY

After I graduated in 1969 I did a secretarial course. That was the accepted route for a girl to take into a career, then: you did your degree, then you learnt how to type and take shorthand.

I wanted to go into journalism, and it was relatively easy to get into in those days. It was opening up for women, like everything else. At that stage, you still needed shorthand for journalism, so I did a course. I learned touch-typing too, and languages. It was great. I worked for the *Worcester Evening News*. The union rate set the same standards for men and women, so there was no discrimination in my pay. I also felt that I was on a par with my employers. There was no overt hierarchy, no forelock-tugging.

I spent the last three years of the sixties working for the *Spectator* in Gower Street, and I thought I'd gone to heaven. Work pretty well stopped at six, when the bottles of Teacher's came out in the editor's room. The editor then was Nigel Lawson, subsequently Chancellor of the Exchequer, and it was wonderfully friendly and convivial and nice, and literary. And although I was only paid £750 a year, it seemed like gold to me, because I was enjoying every second of it.

For my first job I wore very straitlaced, 'secretarial' clothes. I had long hair and wore it up in a backcombed, lacquered bun, because I thought that was what you did, until my boss said he couldn't stand women who put their hair up into buns. So I let it down, and never put it up again. We literally let our hair down in the sixties!

I wore a crimplene dress to my first teaching job in 1969. And I tied my long straight hair back with a shoelace. Such an old-fashioned, schoolmarmy thing to do. But I felt I had to conform to society when I started work.

Offices in the sixties were primitive compared with today. Hardly any had photocopying machines, so you had to use carbon paper between sheets of paper. If you made a mistake you had to rub them out and put a little piece of paper in between each sheet of carbon to type over it. And you did have to dress neatly. Women just didn't wear trousers in those days, not to work.

Sixties weddings – and beyond

The social climate was beginning to change. Girls no longer felt the same obligation to get married as soon as possible or risk being stigmatized as 'left on the shelf'. Nevertheless, shotgun marriages were still common, and the concept of women consolidating a career before getting married and having children was still fairly new. Many of us who did marry and start families in the sixties were conscious of missing out.

We had a good wedding. We'd all always said we'd never get married in a church, man, and all my friends did. But we were living in a crappy flat in Pimlico, and our local registry office was Caxton Hall. So we got married in

Caxton Hall. I was wearing an Empire-line purple corduroy dress from Fenwicks, which I edged with a gold braid. And I bought Chris a white suit, so he got married in white.

When we got married in 1969 we were both twenty-two, and I thought at the time how old we were. Now of course it seems so very young, doesn't it? I would be horrified if my own kids got married at that age.

We had two flats, one very little used. Mainly for parental purposes, but also for the landlord. We were paying £3/15s for one and £3/5s for the other. That was a lot of money in those days. That's partly why we got married in 1969: we were able to give up the £3/5s one.

I wasn't game to live with my boyfriend 'in sin', as it was known then, because I thought it would upset my parents. So we got married. It was very fraught, because we did it fairly quickly and my mother was in a total rage.

My son was born in 1968, and from then on the sixties sort of ended for me. That was it. I remember feeling a bit resentful that being a mother seemed to cramp my style a lot more than being a father did my husband's. And thinking, this isn't fair, I hadn't thought about this.

Women couldn't have babies then go straight back to work in those days. Even in London, there was hardly any organized childcare.

Politics

I remember hearing about Sharpeville, and Rhodesia. They were my first taste of world news. Television was so important in making us aware of what was going on. We might not have understood what was happening, exactly, but we got the gist and we were at least aware of the names. Whereas before, we hadn't had a clue.

Boycotting South Africa and not eating South African fruit was big in our house; my Uncle Tom got the film of the Sharpeville massacre out of South Africa. I went to a lot of demonstrations about that.

I remember the Cuban Missile Crisis of 1962 vividly, genuinely thinking that the world was going to end. Every night the news would come on with a map, showing how far the Russian ships had got towards the American blockade. You could predict the number of days it would take them to reach it. I remember thinking, I ought to do things now, because if the world is blown up I won't get the chance. The sense of relief was amazing, astonishing, when the Russians turned the ships back.

We were all very frightened about the Cuban Missile Crisis at the youth club one night. But it didn't stop us having our chips on the way home. I remember standing outside the chip shop discussing the end of the world. We thought Khrushchev was going to bomb the western world and that would be the end of it, wouldn't it? So you might as well have a bag of chips.

I remember being outraged when Harold Macmillan was suddenly ill and went, and everyone knew that Butler would be the next prime minister – and then somewhere, from some other world, they wheeled out the fourteenth Earl of Home, and he became prime

JUNE 21, 1963   ATLANTIC EDITION

CIVIL RIGHTS: THE MORAL CRISIS
"It is time to act in all of our daily lives."

TIME

THE WEEKLY NEWSMAGAZINE

BOBBY KENNEDY

minister. I was fifteen or so; there was Kennedy in the States who looked like a million dollars; and I thought, what a tired, pathetic, old country this is. I also thought this isn't right, this is not right, that the person who is in charge of our country a) is a lord, b) is a skeleton, and c) looks about 300.

I voted for Ted Heath the first chance I got. It was because I desperately wanted to be different, and everyone was very leftie at school. So I just went in the opposite direction. My idea of rebellion.

I can remember Nelson Mandela being imprisoned when I was in sixth form. It seemed so appalling.

The Profumo scandal of 1963 was the real change of the sixties. We lapped that up. It meant that what was good for the goose was good for the gander; it was the start of the crack in society.

England was just beginning to 'swing' – well, London was, at least – when the Profumo affair blew up and shocked our small town, because John Profumo was Stratford's MP. It was almost as if someone had written Peyton Place about Stratford and was pointing the accusing finger at all of us. We dug Stephen Ward – decadent, despairing, drugged! He fitted. But Christine Keeler had let our side down.

movements and shakers

Like everyone else, I thought Kennedy was the bee's knees. I wasn't really political, but I thought England was a tired country run by old people, and I thought America was an enterprising, ambitious country run by young people, and Kennedy symbolized that.

In 1964 our school, like hundreds around the country, had a mock general election, with a Labour candidate, a Tory candidate and a Liberal candidate. But we were unique in that we were the only boys' public school that returned a Labour candidate; we even made it into *The Times*.

The common rooms at university, which had been designed originally for drinking lots of beer and playing shove ha'penny, were suddenly covered in notices about Agitprop meetings, and you were expected to demonstrate against this or that politician or nuclear weapons, and so forth. There was quite a lot of action.

Churchill's funeral in 1965 had a huge impact on me. It felt as if it really was the end of an era. I remember people saying, 'Who's going to have the next State funeral? There isn't anyone worth having a State funeral for.' It was like Churchill was the last statesman Britain could produce, and that huge changes were about to happen.

I'd been very religious, then I turned to communism when I was about fourteen. I was a member of the Young Communist League, and went to Youth Parliaments and spoke for the communist cause – in Wimbledon! Bit of a lost one there. The local authority let us use the town hall for Youth Parliaments, it was a really big adventure. You'd go along once a month and sit in the council chamber, and there'd be the Tories,

TARIQ ALI

Tariq Ali was Britain's student revolutionary leader who led the anti-Vietnam demo in Grosvenor Square and edited The Red Mole *magazine.*

"The most amazing moment for me was when I received a little handwritten letter in the post at my college in Oxford, from the great Bertrand Russell – one of the philosophers we'd been studying – asking me to visit him. I went and had tea with him, and he asked me to go to Vietnam on behalf of his committee, and to set up an informal war crimes trial. It was the most incredible moment of my life. And having lived under American bombs for several weeks gave our anti-war demos a certain edge.

Later on, one of the best things was becoming friends with John Lennon after interviewing him for *The Red Mole*. He rang me and said he'd been so inspired by our talk he'd written a little song that we could sing on demos – and he sang it over the phone to me: it was 'Power to the People'. And Mick Jagger wrote me out a copy of his 'Street Fighting Man' too, with a note: 'This is the song the BBC are refusing to play on the radio.' So we published it in the magazine."

...DAYS I'LL REMEMBER...

the Labour Party, the Liberals, and the Communists. Goodness knows how we got in.

When the 1966 election results came in I was down at Trafalgar Square, watching the teleprinter, and people were jumping or being pushed into the fountains right left and centre. It was a bit like the end of World War Two.

One of the good things about university was the number of non-British people there. But I can remember the terrible fights during the Six Day War in 1967. These were people who had previously being doing the same course, and they were now almost having a surrogate war. Palestinian and Jewish students were at each other's throats.

I was involved in the Polaris marches, and the big anti-Vietnam War demonstration in Grosvenor Square. One of my friends was arrested for carrying a placard. A policeman broke it then said it was a dangerous weapon. I got hit over the head with a truncheon. It was very frightening.

In 1968 I went to the anti-Vietnam War demonstration in Grosvenor Square. And the big thing in the press was how the wonderful police horses were being brutalized by the bad guy demonstrators; but I can tell you that actually being charged by mounted police, by a cavalry charge… You'd been brought up to think of police as kind and civilized, helpful bobbies. Inside the demo you thought: these guys are prepared to kill me.

I went to America in 1968, and in Washington there were riot police with guns, shields, and a curfew after 10 o'clock. Another illusion of peace and love shattered. I was involved in a police intervention in a 'happening', and the organizer's wife kept calling the police 'pigs'. All the daffodils and other flowers in our hair would not have made for peace and love that night.

I went to America in 1968. I got a job as a *Sunday Times* researcher on the 'Insight' column for the Democratic Convention in Chicago. There was a counter-culture there, the hippie scene, but they were really serious. They were talking revolution, they were talking Weathermen and bombs. There was an odd mixture of what had been sheer hedonism in England, and a political element, SDS, Black Panthers; terrrifying, in a way. Chicago during the Convention, with the build-up of troops on Michigan Avenue, was the biggest crowd I'd ever been in in my life. I was down in the street opposite the Hilton, and there were people and tanks, and hippie girls putting flowers into gun barrels. I thought, something's going to go very badly wrong here. I had to go up to Newtown where they were tear-gassing students – absolute chaos. Terrifying.

SKETCH SOUVENIR
FIRST MEN ON THE MOON

Daily Sketch

Monday, July 21, 1969   WEATHER: Dry, warm.   55   Price Fivepence

4 a.m. MAN TAKES HIS FIRST WALK ON THE MOON

Neil Armstrong steps from the Moonship in one of the last practice sessions before the mission.

From JOHN STEVENSON, Houston, Monday

MAN took his first steps on the Moon today. The time: 3.57 a.m.—nearly seven hours after Neil Armstrong and "Buzz" Aldrin touched down on the Sea of Tranquillity.

The two astronauts skipped their four-hour rest period to push ahead with the historic walk in the searing heat of the lunar dawn.

Armstrong emerged first, for a walk expected to last 2½ hours. As he left the Eagle spacecraft the temperature outside was around 150 degrees Fahrenheit.

Aldrin, remaining in Eagle for 25 minutes in case of an emergency return by his commander, started to run his 35mm movie camera.

HATCH OPEN

At 3.39 came the dramatic message the world was waiting for: Hatch is open.

"Put your left foot to the right a little" came Aldrin's voice as he directed Armstrong down the ladder.

"Takes a long time to get all the way down, doesn't it?" Armstrong remarked to Aldrin.

"Yeah," Aldrin replied.

First live TV pictures were flashed onto the world's screens at 3.55.

Armstrong's foot was seen poised above the rungs as he climbed down the ladder.

At 3.57 Armstrong stepped on to the moon's surface and said: "That's one small step for man."

Armstrong: "I can see the footprints of my tread in the fine powder.

"It's like a fine layer of powdered

I was in Paris in 1967–68, and it was wonderful realising that this huge mass movement of young people was happening there too. I missed out on the hippie drug thing – everyone was quite normal when I left England, and totally drugged-out when I got back – but I had the revolutionary thing instead. It was the last day to hand my dissertation in and I was running late. I got trapped in the courtyard of the Sorbonne then tear-gassed with student leader Daniel Cohn-Bendit.

They showed the moon landing on a huge colour TV in the foyer of my school, and I remember going to my aunt's place that night in Maidenhead, and while they were on the moon it was a big full moon over London.

RICHARD BRANSON

Richard Branson, global tycoon and balloonist, was a sixteen-year-old fifth-former at Stowe School in the summer of 1967 when he and fellow pupil Jonny Gems founded Student *magazine and ran it from the shambolic basement of the Gems' house in Connaught Square.*

"Getting Vanessa Redgrave to give us an interview was a turning point since we could use her name as a magnet to attract David Hockney, Jean-Paul Sartre, John Lennon, Mick Jagger... Peter Blake, who'd designed the 'Sergeant Pepper' album cover, drew a picture of a student wearing a red tie for our first edition. And by October 1968 all the staff of *Student* joined the march to Grosvenor Square to protest against the Vietnam war outside the American Embassy. I marched alongside Tariq Ali and Vanessa Redgrave. It was tremendously exhilarating to march for something I believed in, with tens of thousands of others. You felt at any moment that things could get out of control. And they did. When the police charged the crowd, I ran like hell. A photograph later appeared in *Paris Match*. It shows me, back arched, an inch away from the outstretched hand of a policeman who was trying to catch me as I sprinted across the square."

...DAYS I'LL REMEMBER...

SATURDAY,
NOVEMBER 23, 1963
THREEPENCE
No. 14840 •

Daily Herald

Jackie cradles her husband after
sniper blasts from window

ASSASSINATED!

They rode in the car through the cheering crowds. The President and his wife. The Governor of Texas and his wife. Then bullets shot into the car. John Kennedy fell to the floor, dying.

Kennedy shot dead in car

From JOHN SAMPSON and ANTONY CURRAH
NEW YORK, Friday

PRESIDENT JOHN KENNEDY was assassinated today as he drove in an open car with his wife, Jackie, through the streets of Dallas, Texas. He was shot through the head by a hidden sniper and died in hospital about 30 minutes later.

Tonight, police in Dallas were holding a Communist, 24 - year - old Lee Harvey Oswald on a charge of killing a policeman in a chase soon after the assassination. He is also suspected of killing Mr. Kennedy.

Oswald, a former Marine, defected to the Soviet Union in 1959, and returned to America last year. Two months ago he was arrested in New Orleans with several Cubans for circulating Communist leaflets.

Two policemen chased him into a Dallas cinema this afternoon. One of the officers was shot dead before Oswald was detained.

Mr. Kennedy, who was 46, was shot from a window on the fifth floor of an office building as he waved to cheering crowds. The bones from a meal of fried chicken were found in the building, indicating that the killer had been waiting there for some time.

THIS IS SUSPECT No. 1

THIS is the man police suspect of shooting President Kennedy.

He is 24-year-old Lee Harvey Oswald, chairman of the U.S. Fair Play for Cuba organisation.

Oswald went to Russia in 1959 and said his departure from America was "like getting out of prison." He asked to become a Soviet citizen.

But the Russians refused permission and he returned to America last year with his Russian wife.

The couple have two children. Mrs. Oswald does not speak English.

'All over'

Police brought her to headquarters in Dallas last night and were preparing a list of questions to ask her.

Oswald has been charged with shooting a policeman who helped to arrest him in a Dallas cinema.

But police have not established whether he was the man who killed the President. Tests are being made for fingerprints on the rifle believed to have been used by the assassin.

Police quoted him as saying "It's all over now" as he was arrested.

Captain Will Fritz, head of the Dallas Homicide Division, told reporters: "He hasn't admitted anything yet, but he looks like a good suspect."

HER RED ROSES

Police said tonight that Oswald was known to have been employed in the building. But he denied any connection with the assassination.

As President Kennedy fell, Governor John Connally, of Texas, riding in the same car, was also seriously wounded.

Mr. Kennedy crumpled face down to the floor of the car. His wife dropped a bouquet of red roses, went down on her knees and cradled his head in her arms, sobbing: "Oh no, oh no."

The car, driven by a Secret Service man, roared off to the nearest hospital, where Mr. Kennedy was given a blood transfusion.

Two Roman Catholic priests were called to his bedside, and administered the Church's Last Rites.

Mr. Kennedy—the fourth American President to be killed in office—is succeeded by Vice-President Lyndon Johnson, aged 55.

Mr. Johnson was sworn in as President at Dallas on the plane which flew Mr. Kennedy's body from the local airport to Washington.

As soon as the brief ceremony was over Mr. Johnson, obviously shaken, turned to officials and muttered: "O K, let's get this plane back to Washington."

Mrs. Kennedy, silent with grief, was at the

Continued on Page Three

Lyndon Johnson takes the oath. By his side, Jackie Kennedy.

THE OATH AT A MOMENT OF GRIEF

A MAN, still half-numbed with shock, utters the words that establish him as President of the United States.

Lyndon Johnson takes the oath on board a plane at Love Field, Dallas.

By his side a grief-stricken Jackie Kennedy.

District Judge Sarah Hughes, weeping, holds the Bible with Johnson.

At the new President's right hand is his wife.

A vow

Soon President Johnson was on his way to Washington in the plane, which also carried the body of John Kennedy.

At Washington the new President spoke briefly of "a loss that cannot be weighed."

And he vowed: "I will do my best. That is all I can do. I ask your help—and God's."

BERLIN MOURNS ON THE MARCH

EIGHTY THOUSAND people gathered around West Berlin's city hall late last night in a demonstration of grief at President Kennedy's death.

Thousands of them had marched with torches. A banner borne above them said: President Kennedy is dead, but he will live in our hearts. He told us: "I am a Berliner."

President Kennedy won West Berlin's heart with those four words when he visited the city in June.

Mayor Willy Brandt, in a voice shaking with emotion, told the vast crowd last night: "I feel as if a light has gone out for all men who hoped for peace and a better life."

IN MOSCOW radio and television programmes were interrupted to give news of the assassination.

Man of peace

The Soviet Communist Party newspaper Pravda praised President Kennedy as a champion of peace. Mr. Kruschev was reported to be hurrying back to Moscow from a visit to Southern Russia.

IN LONDON, the Football League sent out a message to all League clubs calling for a minute's silence before today's matches.

President Kennedy's sister-in-law, Princess Lee Radziwill, heard the news at her London home.

Today she flies to America to be with Jackie, her sister.

President Kennedy's sister, Patricia, wife of actor Peter Lawford, was last night under a doctor's care at her home in Santa Monica, California.

ON WALL STREET share values dropped by £2,000million on the news of President Kennedy's assassination.

THE MOMENT OF TERROR IN DALLAS..

Jackie Kennedy leaps up in the car as the President collapses. A security guard tries to help.

'Where were you?'

The question 'Where were you when you heard that Kennedy had been shot?' (Friday 22 November 1963) has long been a catchcry of the baby boomer generation. It was such a seminal event, nearly all of us can remember where we were, what we were doing. Here's a selection.

Kennedy's assassination was a major event in my life. Mike Scott was on Granada TV's *Scene at 6.30* that Friday evening, and I was getting ready to go to the church youth club. At twenty to seven the phone rang on the news desk, and he picked the phone up and his face went absolutely white, and his mouth dropped open, and he didn't talk, he just listened. You couldn't help but watch, because he was obviously receiving some information that wasn't about the next bit of film being stuck or whatever. He put the phone down and said that information had come out of America that President Kennedy had been shot, and was possibly seriously hurt, but there was no real news about his condition. By twenty past seven, when I left, the news had been announced that he was dead. When I got to the youth club, everybody was crying. I don't think that would happen over a politician today.

My sister and I were getting ready to go to a dance at our school. I was putting on a particularly fetching orange outfit I'd made from an old dress plus some chiffon material I'd got in Spain that summer. Suddenly she burst into my bedroom with the terrible news, all tears and horror. I was a year younger, and far more concerned about the fact that the assassination had ruined the evening. We went to the dance, but it was a very subdued affair. No fun at all.

I was at one of those dances in a village hall. There was a pathetic local rock group, playing sub-Merseysound. We sat around whispering; no one dared talk loud. But it was our Friday night out. We'd waited all week through school for this. Why should our Friday night dance be ruined because he'd been killed?

I was in my studio in Paris, and my Italian boyfriend rang me up to tell me the news. I was so shocked. We all had this fantasy about Kennedy and the new Camelot, didn't we? How they were both so young and glamorous and sophisticated, and into the arts, and different from their predecessors.

I was on my way to a Young Communist League meeting, and when I got there they were all glued to the telly, a tiny black and white set. Even though he was in many ways the enemy, Bay of Pigs and all that, it was beyond that, it was devastating.

Banning the Bomb

I really did think the Bomb would annihilate us all, that life held nothing for us. But I was too young to be allowed to go on the Aldermaston marches, so I marched at the front of the Newcastle chapter instead. It coloured all my thinking.

I remember the party in Burton where I first spotted a guy wearing not only a green parka but also a CND badge. It was the most exciting party I'd ever been to. There and then, in 1963, I promised myself I'd escape to London to be nearer those interesting men who belonged to CND and who lived dangerously. That badge symbolised a whole new intellectual world opening up to me.

My sister and I weren't allowed to go on the whole Aldermaston march, but we did join it for the final day one year. It was just wonderful. It would have been even more wonderful to have marched the whole way, and slept in a huge group in school

I was at Friday Night Club in Jackson's Lane, and someone came in and told us. We all thought something serious was going to happen; that the Russians had probably done it and they'd start fighting each other and that we'd all be called up.

I wasn't aware of anything much, I was just having a good time. I didn't care about Kennedy; it was America, a long way away, and it didn't affect me in the slightest.

halls and churches and things, but that one day was pretty good. Singing 'We Shall Overcome' and chanting and feeling very much a part of an exciting and morally correct movement.

I worried for years that it would be wrong to bring a child into a world that could be snuffed out in a moment. I genuinely thought people having babies were being selfish.

Worry about the bomb really did affect my life. There was a feeling of, it's all going to end soon in a nuclear holocaust, so what's the point of trying? It affected my school life, and my choice of career – or rather, my inability to choose a career. It all seemed so pointless.

The environment

In the bitter winter of 1962-3, I was coming up eighteen and the large lake at school froze over. We skated whenever we could, and it was an absolutely magical start to 1963. The whole of London was locked with massive snowfalls, and all the parks were chock-a-block with alpine mounds of ice, dug off the roads. We tobogganed on Hampstead Heath, and got chilblains.

I remember my uncle reading Silent Spring and talking about it in 1963, so I was aware of those concerns. There weren't any birds left in France, for instance, where my uncle lived, because they'd shot them all or they'd been poisoned by pesticides.

My sister and I met two American guys in Bulgaria in 1964, one of them a complete redneck. He had a four-wheel drive with a pair of antlers strapped to the front, and took us for a drive along the coast, during which he flattened every bit of greenery we came across. I remember thinking, hang on, this isn't right. It was my first lesson in ecology.

I arrived in Manchester in October 1965 and I didn't see it for a month. It was just a pea-soup fog. I had no idea where I was going.

We had to wear masks to walk to school during the smogs, in London.

We'd heard about that stuff they were dropping on Vietnam, and we wondered what that was going to do, but I don't think I was any more concerned about that than about Vietnam itself.

GYLES BRANDRETH

Gyles Brandreth, writer and broadcaster, was president of the Oxford Union in 1969 and later became a Tory MP.
"My problem with the sixties is that I remember it all with alarming clarity. As a decade it was completely wasted on me. I wasn't just a middle-aged teenager: I was positively elderly! My political heroes were Harold Macmillan, Sir Alec Douglas-Home and (God save the mark!) Edward Heath. Paul McCartney I met, but I still preferred the songs from 'Salad Days'. In 1968, when the students were manning the barricades, I went to Paris – not to join them, but to take tea with the Aga Kahn for the student magazine *Isis*.

In December 1969 I presented a TV show for ITV called *Child of the Sixties*. I sat on a stool and quizzed the great and the good of the day (Iain Macleod, Michael Foot, etc) about the great moments of the decade. I think the producers had hoped for a hip representative of the now generation. What they got was a know-it-all 21-year-old who thought he was Robin Day (without the bow-tie) with the mindset of Neville Chamberlain.

I do remember being offered a joint and declining it primly. I don't remember being offered free love – are you surprised? The point is: the sixties – I was there, but I wasn't, if you see what I mean. I've a feeling there may have been quite a few like me..."

...DAYS I'LL REMEMBER...

I think, for me, the sixties had nothing to do with anything that happened outdoors at all. Everything happened indoors. You were either in a flat or a house, a pub or a bar, a concert hall or a dance hall, or a lecture hall. Anything that happened outdoors – except sport – was anathema, it had nothing to do with our lifestyle at all.

Women's Lib

It took a long time to filter through to some of us. I mean, even though we'd been brought up to expect much more than our mothers had out of life, we still thought Benny Hill was funny, still thought it normal and acceptable for men to get better jobs than women. Until we hit the job market, and discovered that most of the male managers were far thicker than their secretaries (us, essentially).

When we were still at school we didn't want to be like the spinster schoolteachers, or what we still called 'blue stockings'. No girl dared mention the word career because 'career girl' was still the worst label to get thrown at you.

I went to a very strict, private girls' school, not at all academic, although I'm amazed at how much they taught us at the end of the day. But none of us was expected to take A-levels; it was assumed that we would leave school after O-level, dabble in something, then get married to rich men. You could be a nurse or a teacher for a while, but you weren't expected to have a career.

The summer before I left home to go to university, I remember looking out of my bedroom window into the office next door. I would stare at the girl sitting in there typing. She'd been at school with me, a bright girl who'd got her A-levels. Now she sat there at the typewriter with a big diamond ring glittering in the sunlight on her left hand. She was engaged. Her life now meant being in a secure job, eating sandwiches to save for the mortgage, and looking adoringly into her fiancé's eyes. I didn't want to know about any of that.

The worst thing about the mini skirt was it made you look like a little toy girl, just there to please men. Guys used to call us 'chicks' and 'birds', which I always hated.

I did wonder, in the mid-sixties, why the girls on the counter in the department store got eight pounds a week and the young guys got twelve pounds, for exactly the same work. It's funny looking back and thinking of working for unequal pay without a quibble.

As I became more political, I became aware that my mother was paid two-thirds of a man's wage in the factory, for doing the same job as the man sitting next to her.

One of the things that really bugged me in the sixties was that girls were expected to buy their rounds in the pubs the same as blokes, but we only ever had halves of bitter. I used to think, hang on, we should only have to buy half as many rounds, because all the blokes drank pints.

Quite a few pubs wouldn't let women in. Even when they did, they didn't allow women to drink out of pint glasses. There were ladies' glasses, like goblets, and if a woman wanted a pint the barman would pour out two halves into these goblets. My father would buy me two halves, but he wouldn't buy me a pint.

I remember being thrown out of – or, rather, turned away from – the Savoy for wearing trousers. This must have been about 1967–68.

My parents never encouraged me to have a career. It was seen as a complete indulgence for a woman to go to university because women's careers weren't considered important.

I was unsympathetic to the women's movement when it started, because I thought they just wanted a bigger slice of the capitalist pie, when in my opinion the whole pie recipe ought to be changed. My view was a hangover from the simple hippie lifestyle thing.

The class system

I suppose I was quite bitter when I was young. I had a bit of a chip on my shoulder. I was from a very working class family – I was the first person in my family to stay on at school after the age of fifteen. I might have been a bit bolshie, a bit difficult. I still feel that way now, I still spend half my time at work feeling angry, feeling 'I can take you'.

I developed my idea about class enemies very early; I hated loads of people. I read things like Trotsky when I was about fourteen – people did, then. I can't imagine fourteen-year-olds reading stuff like that now. It made me angry.

In the early sixties, the class system remained absolutely intact. We moved to Essex in 1964, thirty miles outside of London, and my mother's daily cleaning lady – who always called me 'Young Sir' – had never been to London. Her husband always tugged his forelock.

movements and shakers

When it got to about 1965, you began to get this extraordinary new mix of older, quainter aristocracy, who became suddenly pop, and pop became the new upper class. You had characters like Tara Browne, one of the heirs to the Guinness fortune, who was killed in Whitehall when he crashed his car; he was great friends with the Rolling Stones. The mix of the old world, where people lived in big country houses and the squire had a butler, and the new order of pop stars, still held even at the end of the sixties. Having a title was still terribly important, and pop stars bought big country houses and aspired to be lords of the manor.

There's no way Noël Coward was an ordinary guy, but suddenly here's Cilla Black, the Stones, Cathy McGowan, all fundamentally ordinary people just like you and me, becoming celebrities. We all felt just one step away from stardom, which was a hideous lie.

In the sixties we were all liberal and left-wing and we didn't believe in class and we all favoured the idea of comprehensive schools. But the fact is that the scene at the Oxford college balls was one of the old middle-class meritocracy in their evening dresses and dinner jackets down on the dance floor, looking pretty posh, and up on stage were the representatives of the new rebellious working class, who dressed down, looked crazy, drank on stage and were no doubt doing other things as well. They represented freedom and subversiveness to us.

Because of the relative narrowness of communications, what you had is an enormous cultural cohesion. The Beatles and the Stones were recognized and loved nationally. Everybody under a certain age liked them.

There wasn't this fantastic difference between people who liked hip-hop and garden and hothouse and garage and the this, that and the other that you have now. Everybody under twenty-five had to watch *Ready, Steady, Go* on Friday night, and there was a shared injection of excitement, which went all around the country. The young were pulling together, possibly for the first time in history.

We were all pulling away from the Establishment. I was brought up in this very poor working class home, but my mother voted Tory. The stock she came from was very much the deserving poor: they kept their children clean and did well for themselves, all had little businesses and went up the scale a bit. I remember her eyes glazing over as I tried to instruct her in the ways of socialism.

I think there was a lip service to being democratic. It was playing at it. It was a big shock to realize that the class system wasn't breaking down after all. I'm astonished now how little alliances have shifted over the years. But it felt as though it was going when the Labour Party got in, and everybody, all the Hons and such, were thrilled. Except they weren't, really.

ED STRAW

Ed Straw is the chairman of Relate (the Marriage Guidance Council).
"The sixties were our world, our time, an end to more mind-numbing mores than I care to recall. The contrasts were stark. Leaving a traditional public school (an emotion-free zone) and growing long hair and a moustache. Jimi Hendrix struck the first chords of 'Hey Joe' on *Top of the Pops* and my soul said hello. Freedom, power, invention, genius. Was it only jealousy which provoked the later knocking of such heights?"

...DAYS I'LL REMEMBER...

Sport

The 1966 World Cup was magic. But watching the final I assumed, sadly, that it was another world war. When the Germans equalized I thought that was absolutely bloody typical of them. I remember the Russian linesman, and the tension waiting for that decision. But the thing I most remember, along with everyone else, is Kenneth Wolstenhome saying, 'The people on the pitch think it's all over. It is now.' I thought at the time, what a brilliant thing to say. Ever since then, commentators have been trying to say something equally memorable so they will go down in posterity.

I went to the quarter-final between Uruguay and somebody. After about ten minutes Uruguay had eight men; three had had a fight and been sent off. I had a complete sense of betrayal, because you'd gone to this big match and it was ruined.

There weren't many people on the streets when England was playing games in the World Cup. It was a great time, wasn't it? Until the next World Cup, when we just went back to normal.

Being in Manchester when Best, Law and Charlton were playing for United was amazing. You were looking every week at the three best players in Europe. George Best was the first player to take football further than sport and become a fashion trendsetter, sponsoring products and making millions. He was a first, just like the Beatles and Dylan. A product of the times.

I think Gary Sobers is one of the best human beings ever to have lived. And to have seen Gary Sobers play…I found county cricket in those days a bit too slow. At Lord's, there'd be about three people in a ground that could hold 50,000. Rain always stopped play, and there'd be no result. It was deadly dull. So the one-day games made cricket much more attractive to people like me.

I remember when Cassius Clay fought Henry Cooper at Wembley Stadium and Cooper came very close to winning. He belted Clay with a left hook and put him on his pants. But the bell went and there was a huge delay while a mysterious split glove was replaced, and Clay had time to recover. Cooper used to get cut very easily, and Clay managed to open a huge cut over one of Cooper's eyes and that was it. Cooper got a shot at the title a couple of years later, this time at Arsenal Stadium, but again got cut around the eyes. Elizabeth Taylor and Lee Marvin were at the ringside and they got splattered with blood.

Moving on

Although the sixties didn't really turn into the seventies until about 1973, by the end of 1969 we knew times were changing again. After Woodstock came Altamont – for many, a symbol of the death throes of the Swinging Sixties.

Although I was unaware of the passing of an era, I was very much aware of the end of the sixties because halfway through 1969 I finished college and had to face the real world for the first time. It was like the end of the best party ever held. I started a job on 1 January 1970, and nothing was ever as carefree and intoxicating again. The whole world suddenly felt like the morning after.

Universal Electronic Vacuum – hip or what? – which cost about £500 for a set of ten. And I remember someone coming and buying a set, and I said how do you want them framed, and they said, oh no, they were going straight into storage as an investment. That was the moment I realized the whole thing was turning.

In summer 1967 I worked a harvest, and one of the farms had an old guy who still made sheaves. Where we lived in London, there was still a lamp-lighter who rode a bicycle around, lighting the gas lamps. Steam trains died out in the sixties; the Evening Star was the last steam locomotive built in England. All the branch lines disappeared. A whole lot of things vanished, a whole society, a whole culture.

We had the most wonderful parties and happenings at the art gallery where I worked. That was the way it was, wasn't it? Lots to drink, lots of food, lots of money sloshing around; 'let's have a good time'. It was just extraordinary, the amount of fun it was. But I remember when it all died for me, at the end of the sixties. We'd published a big set of wonderful prints called

For me, the end of the sixties was the end of student life, and the beginning of a married life and a career as a teacher. A very significant change.

recipes with Nimble bread.

So many diets are based on substitutes for proper food.
Nimble is delicious, real fresh bread, but bread baked lighter so it's designed to fit neatly into a calorie-controlled diet—and so to help you slim.
But because Nimble tastes so good, it's bread that the whole family will enjoy—especially toasted for breakfast—yet one slice of Nimble contains only 40 calories, compared to 67 for ordinary bread.

Nimble only 40 calories a slice

is a lovely way to slim

All good things come to an end, don't they?